Hunting Whitetails by the Moon

Text and Photography by

Charles J. Alsheimer

Edited by Patrick Durkin

Published by

krause
publications

700 E. State St. • Iola, WI 54990-0001
Telephone: 715/445-2214
fax: 715/445-4087
World Wide Web:
www.deeranddeerhunting.com

Please call or write for our free catalog of outdoor publications. Our toll-free number to place an order or obtain a free catalog is 800-258-0929. Please use our regular business telephone 715-445-2214 for editorial comment or further information.

Library of Congress Catalog Number: 99-63748
ISBN: 0-87341-813-1
Printed in the United States of America

Photography by Charles J. Alsheimer

Deer & Deer Hunting is a registered trademark of Krause Publications Inc.

Dedication

For Aaron:

You're the greatest son any man could hope to have. For the past 21 years we've had a storybook relationship as a father and son. Together we've climbed to the top of the Rockies, bushwhacked our way through Alaskan tundra, canoed the Everglades to the Atlantic Ocean, explored many of the wild haunts in North America, and spent untold hours in the whitetail forest. It's been a special trip.

You're one of the greatest joys in my life. Thanks for loving me, thanks for being there, and thanks for the memories.

Contents

Acknowledgments

The past two decades have gone by too fast. I often reflect on my life and think how blessed I've been to have a job that I once could only dream of having. Something I've learned in my half-century on Earth is that life pretty much boils down to a collection of memories — because the present is much too brief. It's the memories of things, places, times and people that have made my life a blessing.

In assessing the path I've taken, I'm grateful and indebted to those who have made my trip possible. I once heard a person say, "A man who fails to remember his past has no future." Well, thanks to those who have given me a wonderful past, the future looks bright. At the risk of leaving someone out I'd like to salute a few people who have helped make my life's journey, and this book in particular, a joy.

Carla: To the love of my life, I say thanks. You've made it possible for me to fly — you gave me my wings, kept me on course, and encouraged me all along the way. Thank you for being a wonderful wife and my best friend.

Wayne Laroche: Thanks for turning on my lunar light bulb five years ago. You're the most down-to-earth, common-sense wildlife biologist I've ever met. Your way of making the complex understandable never ceases to amaze me. You've been a great coach.

Patrick Durkin and Debbie Knauer of *Deer & Deer Hunting*: You're two of the greatest magazine people in the world — the best. Thanks for giving me the platform to share what I've learned, and thanks for always being there.

Paul Daniels: Thanks to one of my best friends in the world. You've always been willing to do anything I've needed — from modeling to caring for the deer operation. I love ya, man!

Terry Rice: Thanks for all the early-morning modeling sessions. You're great at what you do and your friendship means a lot to me.

Bob and Alma Avery: Without your love and the opportunities you gave me to observe deer on your wilderness paradise, I might never have been able to witness the moon's impact on whitetails.

Ben Lingle: Thanks for giving me one of my first breaks in this business. Access to your estate gave me some incredible insights into the world of the whitetail.

Tom Morgan and Dave Griffith: Thanks for sharing your whitetail insights. You are two of the best whitetail breeders in the business.

Mike Biggs, Leonard Lee Rue III, and Erwin Bauer: Over the long haul, you guys have been the crème de la crème of whitetail photographers. Thanks for inspiring me and keeping my competitive fire lit. Most of all, thanks for being my friends.

Jim, Charlie, Jack, Aaron, Paul, Whitey, Spook, Carla, and Buttercup: Without you, I wouldn't have learned what I know about whitetails. Collectively you have taught me more than all the wildlife biologists or scientific journals combined. Thanks for allowing me a window to the whitetail's hidden world.

Last, but most importantly, I want to thank Jesus Christ for the gift of life. To some, the mere mention of His name is a turn-off. To others, He is looked at as a crutch. But to me, He is the reason for living, the reason for hope, the reason for the successes I've had. I owe what I have today to the Grace of God. It's that simple. I serve a great and loving God and without Him none of this would be possible.

Introduction

What does the whitetail mean to you? Have you ever thought what your life would be like if whitetails weren't part of the natural world? Chances are, North America's favorite deer evokes a million different feelings within hunters across this great continent. The white-tail inspires and addicts at the same time. Why else would we sit in a tree stand for hours in the most miserable conditions? Through rain, sleet or snow, deer hunters keep coming back for more.

I hate to think what my life would have been like without the white-tail. This animal truly introduced me to nature. My childhood fire was lit by the graceful figure of a mature buck running across a plowed field on our farm. That fire has kept me heading back to the woods for more than 45 years.

In my wildest dreams I never envisioned writing a book like this. But the curves in my life's journey brought me to this point. You see, I've gone through a process of sorts in my relationship with the whitetail. When I was a boy, all I ever wanted was a glimpse of a deer. Then, during my teen-age years, the thrill of hunting whitetails was a big part of my life. As I climbed the hill of life, I went from being a young man to middle-aged. In the process, the way I viewed life and the things around me changed. The thrill of the hunt took on a new dimension: the desire to know all I could about whitetails.

I still love to hunt, but during the past 10 years my focus has changed from the hunt and the kill to understanding the whitetail's many myster-ies. This quest for knowledge has taken me down many side roads and, for the most part, all have been fascinating. Some have turned out to be dead ends, and some just faded into the forest.

Other trails have enriched me beyond measure. One such trail is how the moon influences white-tailed deer movements. It's been a special trip.

During the thousands of hours I've huddled behind a camera and sat in a deer stand, I've come to realize how little we know about this great animal. In the text that follows, it's my hope that I can shed some light on the mystery of how the moon affects deer movements.

I hope you enjoy the journey.

— *Charles J. Alsheimer*
August 1999

Things to Remember

○ *Fine-tuned deer herd:* This is critical for the rut to be noticed. When the adult doe-to-buck ratio is greater than 3-1, rut behavior will likely be limited.

○ *Lunar Cycle:* One lunar cycle, from new moon to new moon (when the moon is dark), is completed in 29 days, 12 hours, 44 minutes and 2.8 seconds.

○ *Autumnal Equinox:* When there is 12 hours of daylight and 12 hours of darkness in fall. This is usually on or about Sept. 23 each year.

○ *Pre-Rut Moon:* This is the first full moon after the autumnal equinox. In previous articles in *Deer & Deer Hunting* magazine, this moon was called the harvest moon. To avoid confusion, we'll refer to the harvest moon as the pre-rut moon. In parts of the North and South, some does enter estrus after this moon.

○ *Rutting Moon:* This is the second full moon after the autumnal equinox. In previous articles in *Deer & Deer Hunting* magazine, this moon was called the hunter's moon. To avoid confusion, we'll refer to the hunter's moon as the rutting moon. This moon kicks off the rut in the North. From this full moon through the third-quarter moon, bucks will be in their seeking/chase phase.

○ *Post-Rut Moon:* This is the third full moon after the autumnal equinox. In the North, 10 percent to 15 percent of the doe population is often bred at this time. In various parts of the South, many does will enter estrus after this moon.

○ *Seeking Phase of the Rutting Moon:* This period typically begins three to four days before the rutting moon and ends two to three days after this full moon. This is when bucks actively seek estrous does. This period will overlap the "Chase Phase." Scraping can be intense during this time.

○ *Chase Phase of the Rutting Moon:* This period begins about two days after the rutting moon and lasts three to four days into the "Breeding Phase." This is when bucks chase nearly every doe they see in an attempt to find one in estrus. In herds with good age structure and well-balanced doe-to-buck ratios, scraping is intense during this time.

○ *Breeding Phase:* The prime breeding window begins about seven days after the rutting moon. It lasts for about 14 days. During this time, 70 percent to 80 percent of mature does will be bred. The end of scraping activity indicates this phase has begun.

○ *Rut:* A general term that refers to the period covering the seeking, chasing and breeding phases. In fine-tuned herds, this period normally is intense for about 25 days. This includes about 10 to 11 days before the breeding phase and 14 days during the breeding phase. The most intense period for buck sightings, chasing, fighting and tending during this time will typically occur one to two days after the rutting moon until three to four days into the breeding phase.

○ *Traditional or Classic Rut:* When the rutting moon falls during the first eight days of November, I believe the rut's intensity is generally greater than it is in years when the rutting moon occurs earlier or later than this period.

○ *Rut Suppressants:* Always be aware that weather, warm temperatures, human pressure, high doe-to-buck ratios (greater than 3-1), changing food sources, and baiting can alter the rut's chemistry and intensity.

CHAPTER 1

Why The Interest?

A respected deer hunter once told me, "The best time to kill the buck of your life will be under a new moon in November when the nights are totally dark."

I'll never forget the words of that white-tailed deer authority. I heard that prediction in my early 20s, and for the next 15 years I heard other deer experts preach similar thoughts. They said a full moon during the rut was the worst time to hunt whitetails. Because of what I read and heard, I worked to ensure I did my serious deer hunting when the moon was completely in the Earth's shadow.

But I've also long believed Longfellow's words: "Things are seldom as they appear to be." I should have taken his words more quickly to heart when deciphering how the rut occurs. Instead, I forced and manipulated my observations to fit the "expert's" ideas. In fact, until 10 years ago, I had no problem believing the dark of the moon — the new moon — in November was the best time to hunt rutting whitetails. I also confess I occasionally wrote that it was the best time to hunt. Then something changed my mind.

How It Began

In September 1981 I began photographing whitetails on the Lingle Estate in the heart of Pennsylvania. Later, in February 1985, I traveled to New York's Adirondack Mountains to photograph wintering whitetails in several popular yarding areas. While there I met Bob Avery, a legendary Adirondack resident. His family owns a huge parcel of land in this remote region, and part of it is loaded with deer.

Each year I spent more time at the Lingle and Avery properties, photographing spring through winter. In the process, I realized the whitetail's breeding didn't occur the same time each year. My firsthand observations contradicted old advice, as well as scientific research I might have taken too literally.

From 1961 to 1968, New York's Department of Environmental Conservation sponsored a study by Lawrence Jackson and William Hesselton, both senior wildlife biologists. By using the embryos from 864 dog- and road-killed white-tailed does of various ages, the research-

This buck has smelled a doe's urine and is lip-curling, or Flehmening, to determine if the doe is in estrus and ready to breed. Peak breeding can vary from early November to late November, depending on the year.

ers determined the breeding dates of whitetails across New York state. The whitetail's gestation period is roughly 200 days. Therefore, once researchers determined the embryo's age, they could pinpoint a doe's breeding date. Their research put the peak breeding date for New York whitetails at Nov. 15 to 20 each year. What validated this research for me was that it fit research results from other Northern states.

Knowing these results and what I had seen myself, I began looking more closely at data I had collected over the years. By documenting events on film, and keeping and reviewing detailed journals, I found that peak breeding occurred in early November some years. In other years, it didn't happen until mid-November. In still other years, it didn't happen until late November. At first I shrugged off the fluctuations as flukes.

About the same time, I began conducting deer hunting seminars across the country, and soon realized that what I was seeing was more than quirks. Other hunters reported similar observations. A question I frequently heard at my seminars was this: "Why does the rut seem early some years and late others?" Little did they know I had been asking

As the rut progresses, sparring and fighting between bucks intensifies. Once the rutting moon is near, hunters will start seeing increased buck movements.

myself the same question.

In 1989 I began doing some serious long-distance hunts for whitetails. I scheduled these out-of-state hunts for full-moon periods so I could hunt my home farm in New York during November's new moon, when nights were dark.

That revealed another coincidence, or so I thought. During several road trips I killed an exceptional whitetail, and each big buck fell during the full to third-quarter moon. In nearly every case the hunting was incredible, and I saw many big-racked whitetails. Then I experimented and tried an out-of-state Northern hunt under the dark November new moon. It was nearly a bust! Though I killed a big buck, I only saw 14 whitetails in eight days of hunting. Thinking it was a fluke, I tried hunting the new moon in other prime locations, but the results were similar. In checking old journals, I found parallels when I tried to hunt under November's new moon with a camera, gun or bow. I saw deer, but not the same volume as under full-moon periods.

A Historical Basis

I found another piece of information about that time. My home area in

Within days of the rutting moon — the second full moon after the autumnal equinox — most does will enter estrus and be bred. Bucks will sometimes spend every moment of the day scouring the countryside for a willing doe.

western New York is steeped in Indian tradition. The 500-acre potato farm where I grew up contained the site of a former Indian village. Over the years, various artifacts were uncovered. These finds intrigued me in the ways the Iroquois nation lived and hunted. Though modern man tries to take credit for many deer-hunting tactics, the truth is that American Indians mastered decoying, grunt calls, and yes, hunting by the moon, long before Europeans landed on this continent.

American Indians knew all about the best times to hunt rutting whitetails. In talking to historians, and archaeology and history buffs, it's apparent that designations like "harvest moon," "hunter's moon," "pre-rut moon" and "rutting moon" came from American Indians. Because their survival depended on knowing the best times to hunt, they mastered how the moon affected deer movements, especially during breeding time, which I call the rutting moon.

The Rutting Moon

American Indians demonstrated their knowledge of animal behavior

Once full-blown breeding begins in the herd, hunting can become difficult because bucks will be locked onto does and move only when the does move. After many years of observation, I now believe the does' estrous cycles are linked to lunar activity.

by the way they named the full moons. For example: the Dakotah Sioux gave two names to the year's 11th moon: "Moon when Horns Are Broken Off" and "Moon When Deer Copulate." British Columbia's Kutenai tribe called the 11th moon the "Killing Deer Moon." The Northern tribes knew what to expect when the rutting moon arrived, and they took advantage of the whitetail's vulnerability.

I slowly realized the things I had been taught about November's full moon were not always correct. Therefore, I went back to my photo files and matched the types of behavior I had photographed with the moon phase. This task wasn't difficult because I've documented the dates of nearly every deer photo I've taken the past 20 years.

By the end of the 1994 deer season, I knew for sure I was onto something interesting. After 10 years of intensive deer photography and hunting across the North, I believed the rutting moon — the second full moon after the fall equinox — was greatly influencing when does entered estrus and were bred. I also believed the behavior of rutting bucks — scraping, seeking, chasing and tending — was heavily influenced by the doe's estrous cycle.

Defining the Terms

One of the most difficult aspects of writing about the pre-rut moon and rutting moon is making everything understandable. In the chapters that follow I'll relate both of these moons to the autumnal equinox, which occurs in late September. In previous articles in *Deer & Deer Hunting* magazine, I always referred to the first full moon after the autumnal equinox as the "harvest moon," but to avoid confusion, I now refer to it as the "pre-rut moon." In those *D&DH* articles, I also referred to the second full moon after the autumnal equinox as the "hunter's moon," but I now refer to it as the "rutting moon."

Purists will note that the harvest and hunter's moons are usually, but not always, described as the first and second moons, respectively, after the autumnal equinox. For the record, the widely accepted definition of harvest moon is the full moon closest to the autumnal equinox (*Farmer's Almanac* and various dictionaries).

Had I gone by that definition, however, the concepts in this book would not have been as easily understood. Why? Every eight to 12 years the harvest moon (pre-rut moon) occurs just before the autumnal equinox, thereby making things difficult to understand.

Maybe I'm giving you more explanation of these definitions than you care to receive. If so, let's just remember the crucial basics: The pre-rut

Rubs like this are prime indicators of what can be found in a mature buck's core area. Contrary to what some hunters believe, I think big bucks are most vulnerable during November's full moon, not the new moon when nights are pitch black.

moon is the first full moon after the autumnal equinox, and the rutting moon is the second moon after the equinox.

It's relatively easy to plot when these moons will occur each year. In fact, in Chapter 16, I'll plot when the rutting moon will occur each year through 2020. In 2005 and 2013, the pre-rut moon will occur before the autumnal equinox. Therefore, I'll also explain my predictions for the timing of the whitetail's rut-related behaviors those two years.

Public Involvement

Since 1996 I've written several *D&DH* articles dealing with the research Wayne Laroche and I have been conducting on the moon's influence on whitetails. These articles provided a huge forum for sharing my predictions.

A byproduct of these writings has been positive responses from my fellow deer hunters. Each year hunters and respected whitetail research-

Needless to say, this was an exciting moment for me. I rattled in this 160-class Saskatchewan buck during the rut's chase phase in 1996. I shot the deer while hunting during a full moon in November, the rutting moon.

ers across North America have written and called to share their insights into our work. That feedback is always revealing. I've been fascinated by the number of hunters who apparently figured out the importance of the rutting moon long before I started thinking about it. I've become acquainted with hunters from Michigan to Maryland who have plotted moon phases and associated deer activity for years. The more I got into it, the more fascinating it became. What I've learned is that everything I "discovered" was nothing new. In other words, all these insights are not my inventions. I just had the ability and opportunities to put my findings into print.

It's also important to recognize several other studies and commercial products concerning the moon's effect on deer are in progress or on the market. No doubt others will follow. After all, hunters are fascinated with anything that affects the whitetail, be it weather patterns or moon phases.

The latter, however, has intrigued hunters a long time. I'm no different. No matter how much I read or see, I'll always want more information. The studies I've read on the moon's impact on deer movements and breeding are some of the most interesting research I've ever seen.

Many things go through my mind when I recall what I've seen and learned about moon-related deer behavior the past six years. Perhaps the most striking is why someone didn't write up their discoveries sooner.

Then again, as you'll see in the pages ahead, the system isn't foolproof. But with each passing year, I think it will be easier to understand and predict.

Alsheimer's Reminders: ————————

○ *Pre-Rut Moon: The first full moon after the autumnal equinox, which occurs in mid- to late September. Also known as the harvest moon.*

○ *Rutting Moon: The second full moon after the autumnal equinox. Also known as the hunter's moon.*

CHAPTER 2

Those Who Paved the Way, Part 1

W hat is research? Is it the findings of scientists who go around in white jackets with metal clipboards collecting endless pieces of data? Is it defined as years of information jotted down in a 99-cent spiral notebook by a bow-hunter, who studies the information to become a better hunter? Or, is research the insights collected by American Indians over hundreds of years that helped them survive?

Webster's New Collegiate Dictionary gives two definitions for "research." The first is a "careful or diligent search." The second is a "studious inquiry, an investigation or experimentation aimed at the discovery and interpretation of facts, revision of accepted theories or laws in the light of new facts, or practical applications of such new or revised theories or laws."

Therefore, according to Webster's, all three possibilities in the opening paragraph could be considered research. When boiled down, research is whatever definition you choose to use.

Certainly today's research scientists fall into the second part of *Webster's* definition. However, it's my belief that few academic researchers have been able to unravel the mysteries of a white-tailed buck better than the likes of Myles Keller, Mitch Rompola, Greg Miller, Roger Rothhaar, or Barry and Gene Wensel, to name a few. If research were measured by results, these guys would stand at the pinnacle.

So would American Indians. They collected information and learned how to use it. Their survival depended on what they knew — and they knew a bunch. Though recorded history is sketchy, there's no question North America's Indians knew how the moon affected whitetails.

The First Modern Moon Research?

Realizing the interest in whitetails and the moon, Al Hofacker — co-founder and former editor of *Deer & Deer Hunting* magazine —

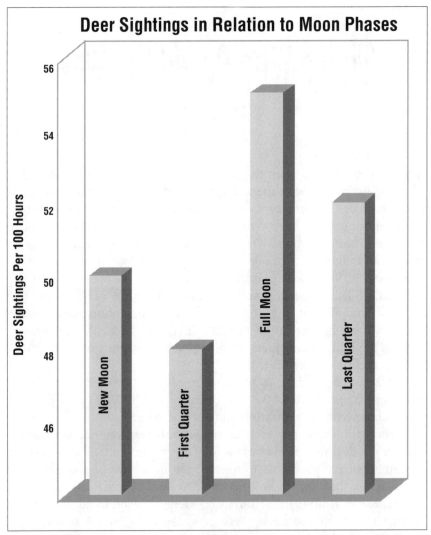

Figure 1: *This chart shows the deer sightings for each moon phase during a four-year observation period reported by* Deer & Deer Hunting *readers in a 1981 survey.*

Deer Sightings by *Deer & Deer Hunting* Readers, 1981

Year	Stand Hours	Deer Sightings	Deer/100 Hours
1977	1,862.25	1,013	54.3
1978	3,809.50	1,776	46.5
1979	3,916.50	1,672	42.7
1980	3,928.75	2,687	68.5

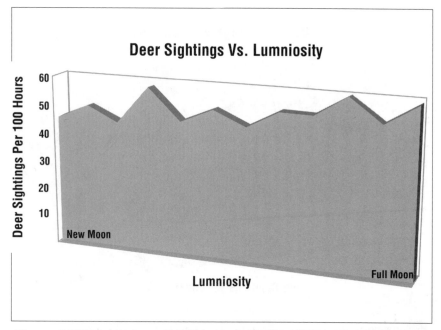

Figure 2: This chart compares deer sightings with the moon's varying luminosity during a four-year observation period reported by Deer & Deer Hunting *readers in a 1981 survey.*

Deer Activity Levels reported by *D&DH* Readers, 1981

Year	*Minimum Activity Occurred*	*Maximum Activity Occurred*
1977	3 Days After New Moon	2 Days Before New Moon
1978	2 Days Before New Moon	First Quarter
1979	1 Day After New Moon	3 Days After Full Moon
1980	3 Day After Full Moon	2 Days After Full Moon

tried to document if the moon had any impact on whitetails and deer hunting in North America.

In the August 1981 issue of *Deer & Deer Hunting*, Hofacker wrote an article titled "The Lunar Cycle and Deer Activity." Hofacker's original intent was to draw on previous writings on the subject. Unfortunately, he found the literature lacking.

Hofacker wrote: "In the scientific literature, deer researchers seldom refer to the moon and its relationship to deer activity. The few researchers who do comment on this topic state that the lunar cycle has no effect on levels of deer activity. However, they present no solid

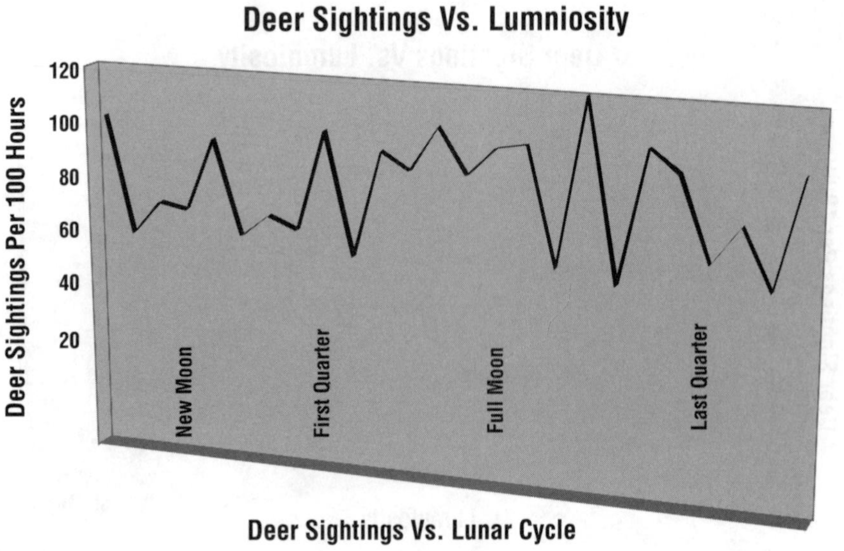

Deer Sightings Vs. Lumniosity

Deer Sightings Vs. Lunar Cycle

Figure 3: This chart compares total deer sightings for each moon phase during a four-year observation period reported by Deer & Deer Hunting *readers in a 1981 survey.*

documentation.

"The popular literature, on the other hand, abounds with references to the moon, its effect on deer activity, and the implications for the hunter striving for optimum results. The consensus of opinion theorizes that daytime deer activity reaches its maximum level in conjunction with the new moon, or the dark of the moon. Conversely, daytime activity declines to its lowest level at the time of a full moon. Again, we are provided with scant documentation."

After digging into the past with little success, Hofacker asked the assistance of the magazine's readers: the Stump Sitters Whitetail Study Group.

This group of volunteers formed in 1977 to collect deer sighting data and share insights and theories involving deer behavior. From 1977 through 1980, stand-hunters in this group collected data on deer sightings. Hofacker used only stand-hunters because he believed the sightings they reported were more likely to represent deer going about their normal activities.

During the Stump Sitters' study, hunters spent 13,516 hours and 45

*During Al Hofacker's four-year research from 1977 to 1980 with **Deer & Deer Hunting's** Stump Sitters Whitetail Study Group, he collected and analyzed more than 13,000 hours of observation data from stand-hunters.*

minutes on stand. They recorded 7,148 deer sightings, for an average of 52.9 deer per 100 hours of stand-hunting.

Hofacker then analyzed his data and broke it down three ways:

○ Deer activity as it related to the four moon phases.

○ Deer activity as it related to the moon's degree of luminosity.

○ The amount of deer activity during the 29-day lunar cycle.

The Analysis

Regarding deer activity vs. moon phases, Hofacker wrote: "Stand-hunting hours were evenly distributed among the four moon phases, ranging from a minimum of 3,262.25 hours (new moon) to a maximum of 3,503.25 hours (first quarter). Compared to the combined

With each passing year, more deer hunters are relying on the moon's influence on whitetails to help plan their hunts and hunting strategies. That influence has long been debated by hunters and writers, but until recently, little research has been done to document lunar effects on deer movements.

average of 52.9 deer per 100 hours, the individual phases of the moon showed no significant differences in deer activity. Minimum deer activity of 50.0 deer per 100 hours (5.5 percent below average) was recorded at the time of the first quarter, while maximum deer activity of 56.5 deer per 100 hours (6.8 percent above average) occurred during the full moon."

Though all the moon phases produced nearly equal numbers of deer sightings, the order of ranking was full moon, first; third quarter, second; new moon, third; and first quarter, last.

In reviewing Hofacker's analysis, I'm not surprised by those results. This is precisely the order of ranking I've recorded for deer

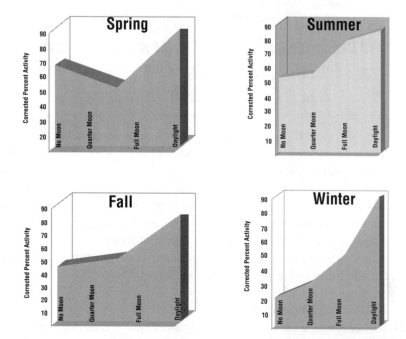

Figure 4: These charts are reprinted from a master's thesis research paper by R. Hood in 1971 at Texas A&M University. They show the effects of light intensity on year-round deer activity. The paper was titled, "Seasonal variations in home range, Movement and activity patterns of white-tailed deer on the Rob and Bessie Welder Wildlife Refuge.

movements in November.

Regarding the moon's luminosity, or its brightness (there are actually 12 degrees of luminosity), Hofacker wrote: "Luminosity is at its minimum at the time of the new moon and reaches its maximum at the time of the full moon. In many cases, two or more days of the lunar cycle have the same degree of luminosity. To cite one example, the luminosity is the same one day before and one day after a full moon. There appears to be a slight increase in deer activity as luminosity approaches its maximum at the time of a full moon."

In looking at Hofacker's illustrations, there appears to be more than 60 deer sightings per 100 hours when there is full or near-full moon luminosity. During the new moon, when there is no luminosity, sightings drop to about 50 per 100 hours.

Regarding the 28-day lunar cycle, the four-year Stump Sitters' study found significant variations in deer activity from year to year.

The erratic sightings Al Hofacker reported in 1981 might be tied to the timing of the rutting moon in the study years. The rutting moon occurred Oct. 27, Nov. 14, Nov. 4 and Oct. 23, respectively, those years.

Hofacker wrote, "If deer activity were closely related to the lunar cycle, one would think the same pattern of increases and decreases would be repeated annually."

Hofacker made this conclusion: "The effect of the lunar cycle on deer activity ... is so minimal that it can probably be ignored as a variable that affects deer activity. Even where fluctuations in deer activity are evident, these fluctuations are not repeated from year to year."

In other words, the Stump Sitters' study was inconclusive in whether the lunar cycle affects daytime deer activity.

A Retrospective Look

Hofacker's research didn't mention two items: First, what percentage of the deer sightings were bucks? Second, what type of movement occurred when the moon was rising or falling?

Hindsight is nearly always 20/20, especially if you aren't the researcher. In looking at Hofacker's data, and interviewing him while writing this book, I see some interesting parallels between his work and current research into the moon's influence on deer.

I believe the reason for the erratic sightings Hofacker reported is tied to the timing of the rutting moon during the study years. From 1977 to 1980, the rutting moon occurred Oct. 27, Nov. 14, Nov. 4 and Oct. 23, respectively. As you'll see in this book, the rutting moon greatly affects when certain deer activity occurs.

Rob Wegner's Research: In The Moonlight

In *Deer and Deer Hunting's* 10th anniversary issue, former editor Rob Wegner wrote an article, "In The Moonlight," in which he revisited the lunar/whitetail relationship. While Hofacker's 1981 article dealt mainly with *D&DH's* research involving its readers, Wegner's 1987 article looked at other research sources, in addition to deer/moon articles in the popular press by various writers and outdoor personalities.

Wegner reprinted many observations, such as these:

Many popular outdoor writers have long believed the full moon is not the best time to hunt deer. Most of them would rather hunt the buck of their dreams when the nights are void of moonlight. I'm not among that group.

"In his book *Deer In Their World* (1983), Erwin Bauer suggests whitetails move more during the early mornings and the late evenings of a new moon. However, he hastens to add that the moon's influence on deer movement remains mysterious and confusing at best, since no solid scientific statistics exist on the question."

"In his 1986 edition of *The Modern Deer Hunter*, John Cartier, a Michigan deer hunter, states this point of view even more emphatically when he insists that deer feel more secure in the open during the dark of the moon. Consequently, the degree of luminosity at night, Cartier tells us, will probably have little bearing on the success of your next deer hunt."

"Byron Dalrymple, the master deer hunter from Texas, argues, unlike Cartier, that during bright nights whitetails feed more avidly than on dark ones. According to Dalrymple, they move around in the moonlight without inhibition. Consequently, the hunter experiences poor hunting at dawn and dusk. By and large, Dalrymple reports, 'the dark of the moon and the small slivers of moon furnish the best hunting.'"

> *'Whitetails during the dark of the moon, if submitted to little or no hunting pressure, often feed during the middle of the day. But ... whitetails can do whatever they need to do with or without the moon or anything else.'*
>
> *— T.S. Van Dyke*

"In his *Stalking Deer* (1986), Don Groves tells us that 'the woods come alive like gang-busters' during the full moon.'"

"No one pursued deer more vigorously on the ridges and in the open glades than T.S. Van Dyke. After observing deer in the moonlight for many years, he offered these words of wisdom: 'Whitetails during the dark of the moon, if submitted to little or no hunting pressure, often feed during the middle of the day. But we must remember that whitetails can do whatever they need to do with or without the moon or anything else.'"

Outdoor Writers vs. Science?

For the most part, many popular outdoor writers have long believed the full moon is not the best time to hunt deer. Most of them would rather hunt the buck of their dreams when the nights are void of moonlight. However, much of the scientific information suggests those preferences are misguided.

According to Wegner's article: "Gary Spencer, a biologist with the Texas Parks and Wildlife Department, reports studies done by the agency found no correlation between lunar phases and nocturnal deer movement. 'We ran a lot of spotlight counts all over Texas and were never able to prove that moon phase or any other factors affected nocturnal deer movements. From personal experiences on spotlight counts, I've seen just as many deer on pitch-black nights as I've seen on a full moon.'

"Edwin Michael, another deer biologist, also arrived at the same results after studying the nocturnal activity patterns of whitetails in South Texas. According to Michael, 'The overall effect of moon phases on deer activity was not statistically significant, and moon phase had no significant effect on deer feeding at different times of the 24-hour period.' He detected no decrease in the number of active deer during daylight of the full-moon phase. His data also indicates the dark-moon phase does not increase the number of deer feeding

I will go to my grave unshakably convinced that the moon phase is critical to a hunter's plans.'
— John Wootters,
Hunting Trophy Deer

during the daytime."

When it comes to respected whitetail authors, few rank with Texas' John Wootters, a mainstay of *Petersen's Hunting* magazine. Wegner quoted Wootters by writing, "John Wootters' advice in his book *Hunting Trophy Deer* (1977), summarizes the consensus in the popular domain: 'I've seen scientific correlations that tended to show the phase of the moon has nothing to do with whitetail activity, if all other things are the same. Which convinces me that either the deer haven't seen the same charts or all other things are never the same. I will go to my grave unshakably convinced that exactly the opposite is true, and that moon phase is critical to a hunter's plans.' Indeed, on no other question do deer hunters and biologists disagree more vehemently."

More Research Needed?

After quoting numerous sources, Wegner concluded his article by writing: "My advice for those deer hunters and/or deer biologists who deny the effect of moon phases on white-tailed deer activity is to spend less time in the lab, the library, and the experimental pens, and more time in the deer forest. I live in the deer forest and my moonlight wanderings indicate that whitetails definitely respond to the lunar cycle."

It's probably safe to say that if a nonhunter were to read what has been written about the moon and whitetails over the years, they would come away shaking their heads. At first glance it all looks murky. However, there's no question that past writings have stimulated research, books and magazine articles.

In fact, I believe much has been done in the 10-plus years since Wegner's moon article to get us closer to unraveling the mysteries of how the moon affects deer movements. In the chapters that follow, I'll share what is being accomplished.

CHAPTER 3

Those Who Paved the Way, Part 2

As the 1980s wound down, more hunters began realizing the importance of the moon's effect on whitetail habits. In the early 1990s, more writers and researchers advanced and promoted several theories, discoveries and moon-related products to help deer hunters. By the end of the 1990s, deer hunters had everything from charts to calendars to books to guide them through the fall's hunt.

Let's look at some more of these people who have paved the way with their lunar insights, as well as some of the tools and devices they developed to help deer hunters.

Richard P. Smith:
Hunting Deer When the Moon Shines Brightly

In January 1994, Richard P. Smith of Marquette, Mich., wrote an article for *Deer & Deer Hunting* magazine titled, "Hunting Deer When the Moon Shines Bright." In this article, Smith referenced several noted deer managers, researchers and hunters.

One person whose thoughts Smith discussed in detail was Alabama physician Robert Sheppard. Sheppard kept computerized records for three large Southern hunting lodges to try to determine the best time to hunt. He also detailed when most bucks were killed. His data included about 30,000 deer sightings and 4,000 kills. Among the things he tracked in his data collection was moon phase.

Smith wrote: "Sheppard found that clients at the three lodges reported seeing more deer from their stands while hunting during the full moon. However, the number of deer harvested was highest during the moon's darker phases.

"The number of deer sighted per hunter day was 5.0 for the full moon, 3.7 for the new moon, 3.7 for the first quarter, and 3.6 for the last quarter. The number of deer killed per hunter day was 0.37 for the last quarter, 0.34 for the new moon, 0.33 for the full moon, and 0.325 for the first quarter. The number of deer killed per hunter day is almost the opposite

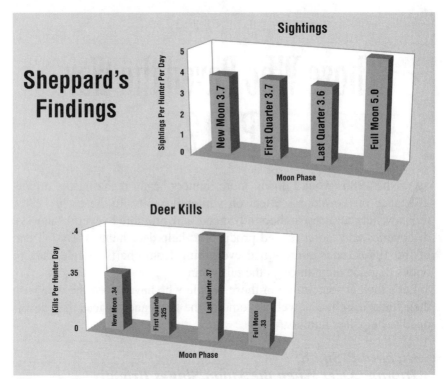

Figure 1: These findings from A. Robert Sheppard appeared in the January 1994 issue of Deer & Deer Hunting *magazine.*

of deer sighted."

Though the harvest figures are a near flip-flop from deer sightings, I believe they're inconclusive because they're nearly the same for each lunar period. In addition, kills — by their nature — contain too many variables. For example, some hunters are more selective, while others tend to shoot quickly if they aren't seeing many deer. That's why I believe deer sightings are the key factors to consider.

However, not everyone Smith interviewed for his article believes deer tend to move more frequently during a full-moon period. Count John Wootters among those who think the new moon (dark nights) inspires more daytime deer activity. This Texan, a well-known author and long-time columnist for *Petersen's Hunting* magazine, has studied and tracked nearly every aspect of whitetails known to man. Therefore, he has his own thoughts on the moon's influence on deer behavior.

Smith wrote: "Wootters is convinced that moon phases affect deer movement. Wootters has kept hunting logs for many years, and now has almost 3,500 deer sightings entered in his computer for a seven- to eight-year period on his 2,000-acre ranch. Wootters reports that he has seen 31.3 percent of those deer during the week of a new moon. Further, 19.3 percent of those sightings were made during the first quarter, and another 19.3 percent were seen during the second quarter. Only 7.1 percent of Wootters' sightings were made during a full moon."

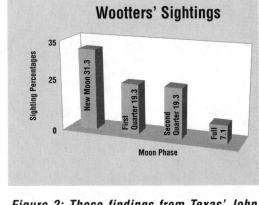

Figure 2: These findings from Texas' John Wootters appeared in the January 1994 issue of Deer & Deer Hunting *magazine.*

Smith quoted Wootters' conclusion from his data. "To sum up, my computer (which knows nothing whatever about white-tailed deer) is telling me that only 7 percent of our deer sightings, over many years of hunting in all weather conditions with rutting intensity ranging from none to 100 percent hot-to-trot, have occurred on days following full-moonlit nights. Yet this represents almost 20 percent of the days in the database. To my notion, that's statistically significant!"

After looking at the works of Sheppard and Wootters, you're almost left scratching your head because they do not agree. The question Smith asked was this: "Is the region of the country playing a part in these differences?" The article suggested Smith found his answer in the published work of Southeastern deer hunter Lynn Ketner. Over a 19-year period, Ketner kept detailed records while hunting Georgia, Tennessee and Alabama. He found the new and first-quarter moon phases each produced 27 percent of his deer sightings. The last quarter and full moon phases each produced 23 percent of the sightings. However, Ketner saw a higher percentage of bucks during the full-moon phase (28 percent) than during any other moon phase.

Obviously, that's significantly more than what Wootters saw on his Texas ranch.

Though Smith's article shed new light on the moon/deer movement theory, there was much more to be learned.

Grant Woods' "Deer Activity Index"

In 1991-92, Grant Woods — a noted South Carolina biologist with a

These items are some of the more popular moon-related guides available to deer hunters in the late 1990s. Upper left is Jeff Murray's "Deer Hunter's Moon Guide," upper right is Grant Woods' "Deer Activity Index," center is Jamie Bulger's "Whitetail Almanac," lower left is Wayne Laroche's "Rut Predictor Chart," and lower right is Deer & Deer Hunting magazine's annual calendar with Laroche's "Rut Predictor Chart."

Ph.D. in deer research — began discussing correlations he found between the moon and the whitetail populations he was managing in Eastern states.

Woods wrote: "I developed DAI using deer activity data collected as part of an ongoing scientific research project. To ensure this research would be meaningful to hunters, only daylight activity data were used to develop DAI. The data were collected by wildlife biologists using standard hunting techniques, primarily while hunting from tree stands. All state regulations and fair chase guidelines were followed. In the six-year period from 1991 to 1996, researchers observed 4,378 wild, free-ranging

Grant Woods' Deer Activity Index is divided into seven activity classes. Each class represents the level of deer activity during daylight, with the number 10 indicating the highest level of activity and 4 indicating the lowest.

deer and harvested 684 of them.

"By working with a national astronomical observatory, I obtained data on several additional characteristics of the moon's orbit that were never before compared to daytime deer activity. These orbit patterns change daily, but the variations cannot be seen by the naked eye. By comparing the astronomical data to a database of thousands of deer observations, statistical tests revealed that some of the moon's orbit characteristics strongly influence daylight deer activity. Two of these characteristics are the moon's declination, which is the angle north or south of the Earth's equator, and its distance from the Earth's surface."

Woods' DAI is divided into seven activity classes. Each class represents the level of deer activity during daylight hours, with the number 10 indicating the highest level of daytime activity and 4 indicating the lowest. The DAI is designed to help hunters and researchers know when to schedule their time afield.

Unlike other products, the DAI does not indicate where to hunt, but rather when to hunt. Also, Woods readily points out that the DAI is not a magic bullet and cannot replace sound hunting techniques.

The DAI can be purchased by contacting Vulcan Outdoors, Box 1847, Birmingham, AL 35201. Phone: 888-760-3337.

Jeff Murray's "Deer Hunter's Moon Guide"

By 1995, outdoor writer Jeff Murray's work concerning his "hunting strategies that revolve around the moon" became increasingly popular. That was the year Murray produced his first "Deer Hunter's Moon Guide" and a book titled *Moon Struck!* Murray says both products are based on scientific writings and hunting observations he and others gleaned from years of hunting whitetails.

Murray's work centers on the belief that the moon's position — i.e., overhead or underfoot — influences how and when whitetails move. He updates his moon guide annually, and tells hunters what time of day they should hunt, and what deer are doing and where they should be hunted.

His book expands upon his guide wheel, and offers insights from

A growing amount of scientific research in the 1990s suggests the moon's position overhead or underfoot does not greatly affect deer movements and feeding activity, but observations from some hunters in the popular press strongly argue otherwise.

himself and others regarding hunting strategies for the various moon phases. His book also details the significance of the full moon that falls during the breeding time. Whether one believes in the moon's relation to deer movements or not, Murray's book is full of valuable information for deer hunters. Murray has a unique way of teasing the reader with what each chapter will offer. For example, Chapter 4, "Moon Times & Food Sources," opens with a poem that starts and ends with these lines: "The Moon's overhead in the twilight sky, the deer are hungry, and so am I. 'Know when deer are feeding?' asks the Man in the Moon, 'I'll tell you right when: Late in the afternoon.'"

For Chapter 6, "Moon Times & Bedding Areas," Murray uses two

Jeff Murray's "Moon Guide" and Jamie Bulger's "Whitetail Almanac" predict when deer will be most active each day and offer advice on where hunters should try setting up to increase their chances for success.

sentences from a poem's beginning and ending to open: "The Moon's overhead in the middle of the day, and you can bet the bedded buck is tucked away. For noontime Moon Time, try the thicket."

Murray's "Moon Guide" and *Moon Struck!* book can be purchased by contacting Fool Moon Press, Box 15013, Duluth, MN 55815. Phone: 800-449-6645

Jamie Bulger's "Whitetail Almanac"

Developed in 1997 by Georgia native Jamie Bulger, the "Whitetail Almanac" is a comprehensive calendar that predicts daily feeding and travel patterns for whitetails.

Bulger said: "Long before 1997 I became very interested in how the whitetail reacted to the moon. After years of studying the subject, I decided to come out with my own aid for hunters. Before developing the Almanac calendar, I was very familiar with other moon guides on the market. It didn't seem many were user-friendly. I decided on a calendar format that provided hunters a visual aid that was easy to understand."

During the hunting months, each day on the Almanac calendar contains information indicating when a major feeding period should occur and where to hunt during that time. The information in the calendar comes from several sources, including Professor James Kroll's landmark work on whitetail movement. Other data came from hunting club observations, input from individual hunters, and Bulger's own observations on how deer patterns are influenced by moon phases and position.

The "Whitetail Almanac" can be purchased by contacting Hunter's Edge, 195 Kelly Road, Bainbridge, GA 31717. Phone: 912-248-6228.

Professor James Kroll

For serious whitetail enthusiasts, James Kroll needs no introduction. Over the years he has been on the leading edge of whitetail research. He has conducted several studies relating to whitetail movement patterns. His book *Solving the Mysteries of Deer Movement* offers a wealth of information, specifically how deer are affected by the moon.

Just before the rut's breeding phase begins, scraping by white-tailed bucks will be intense. Once breeding begins, scraping quickly tails off.

"Try as we have to disprove the hypothesis that the full moon triggers breeding, we have not been able to reject it. We have disproved the hypothesis that moon position has any real effect on activity."
— Professor James Kroll

During 1996 and 1997, Kroll ran a series of articles in *North American Whitetail* magazine using the general theme of "What Makes Deer Move." In the seven-part series he looked at myriad movement triggers. A central point of the articles was how the moon affects deer movement. Several quotes from Part 7 of Kroll's *NAW* piece follow:

1. "In our research at the Institute for White-tailed Deer Management and Research, we discovered that deer have a four- to six-hour feeding activity cycle that is depressed during daylight. The standard activity curve, no matter what the geographic location, is for deer to become increasingly active just about sunset and remain active on a four- to six-hour cycle throughout the night, then become less active at daylight. If the moon position had an appreciable effect on deer activity, this general pattern would shift with moon phase or position, but in our research we have not seen such a shift, only a change in feeding corresponding to the amount of nocturnal light. What we have learned from this and other studies forces us to conclude that moon models, as they currently are being used, are poor predictors of deer activity."

2. "Earlier in this series, we noted how deer cue on the full moon — be it the harvest (pre-rut) moon, the hunter's (rutting) moon or some other moon — to synchronize the rut. If deer in your area are mid-November breeders, the hunter's (rutting) moon is the primary rut cue in operation; the peak of breeding will occur shortly after this full moon. Because there is a lag time between the releaser (full moon) and actual breeding five to seven days later, most breeding activity will occur around the last-quarter moon."

3. "Try as we have to disprove the hypothesis that the full moon triggers breeding, we have not been able to reject it. We have disproved the hypothesis that moon position has any real effect on activity."

Kroll's articles and his book intensely discuss when deer move, both in terms of moon phase and time of day. His research shows the least amount of activity occurs from the first-quarter to the full-moon period.

Wildlife researchers have used radio telemetry equipment to help them try to correlate deer activity with lunar influences.

Also, mature bucks (3½-plus years of age) tend to move during darkness 77 percent of the time, illustrating why they're so hard to hunt.

The highest amount of daytime activity shown in his research occurred during a new to first-quarter moon phase. The second highest level of activity occurred from the full moon to the last-quarter. This information closely parallels what Hofacker discovered in his research, which we outlined in Chapter 2.

Kroll's book *Solving the Mysteries of Deer Movement* can be purchased by contacting the Institute for White-tailed Deer Management and Research, Box 6109, SFA Station, Nacogdoches, Texas 79561.

A Final Thought

In assessing everything that's been written on how deer move in relation to the moon, one thing is clear: few noted writers or researchers agree. While some claim the moon's position is the answer, others say it's the moon phase, its declination or how far it is from the Earth. In

During my past 25 years of extensive photography and hunting, plus raising whitetails for the past decade, I find nothing to be as predictable as deer activity around the rutting moon period and the days that follow.

their writings, scientists Kroll and Woods believe strongly that the moon's position overhead or underfoot is not the key to deer activity, while members of the popular press like Murray and Bulger believe it is. Needless to say, these discussions can get confusing.

Because of my interest in the moon/whitetail relationship, I've looked at everything in the popular literature. I've seen cases where moon position has a definite influence on deer activity, especially when the moon is rising over the horizon at the same time the sun is setting, and vice versa. However, during my past 25 years of extensive photography and hunting, plus raising whitetails for the past decade, I find nothing to be as accurate as the predictability of activity around the rutting moon period and the days that follow.

When it comes to the full moon's influence on the breeding period, Kroll appears to be on the same page as biologist Wayne Laroche, whose breakthrough research will be discussed in detail in the following chapters. Even though Kroll and Laroche have never met, much of their research is nearly in lockstep.

CHAPTER 4

Breaking Through: Wayne Laroche's Research

During my many years of writing about whitetails, I've been fortunate to meet and talk with some of the continent's most respected deer researchers. Al Brothers, Larry Marchinton, Karl Miller, John Ozoga, Bill Severinghaus and Grant Woods are a few of the better known people I've had the pleasure of working with.

However, many other deer fanatics have steered the way I and many others view whitetails. One of these people is Vermont native Wayne Laroche. He's not well known in deer circles, but from the time we met, I realized his affinity for whitetails. Wayne grew up in a deer

Wayne Laroche

hunting family from Sheldon, a small Vermont town. Coincidentally, he and I began deer hunting in 1964, and both of us have actively pursued the whitetail since.

By profession, Wayne is a wildlife biologist. He received his bachelor's degree in wildlife management from the University of Maine in 1972. In 1986, after working several years in various wildlife and fisheries jobs, he earned a master's degree in natural resources from Humboldt State University in California.

I didn't meet Wayne until 1994. Since that time we've shared ideas and information on a host of things relating to whitetails. I've always been impressed with his technical background and his ability to make the complex easy to understand. I've also been impressed by the serious way he hunts whitetails, and his interest in how the moon affects deer.

Make no mistake: I'm not the brains behind what Wayne and I have done in our lunar research. He's the brains, while I do some of the legwork. He

Rubbing behavior remains high throughout autumn, especially if a deer herd contains mature bucks and its doe-to-buck ratio is below 2-1. While Wayne Laroche provides the brains behind our lunar research, I like to think I provide the in-the-field insights provided through my hunting and photography.

knows the scientific end of things, and is adept with computers, light meters and all the other technical aspects of research. Meanwhile, I draw from years of in-the-field experiences and obtain the actual breeding data that helps us make our rut-related predictions.

Whenever I head off on a tangent, Wayne steers me back on the trail. And whenever he wonders about a behavioral aspect of whitetails, I add my 2 cents of insight or reveal a part of the whitetail's life that few others have witnessed. It's been a good working relationship. In the process, I've come to respect Wayne as a biologist and, more importantly, as an individual. In fact, he's one of the best biologists I've had the pleasure of working with.

Why the Interest?

My interest in lunar-related deer behavior began in the late 1980s while hunting and photographing. Laroche's interest began while hunting northern Maine the first week of November 1991. That year, the rutting moon occurred Oct. 22. When he began hunting the first week in November, the woods were torn up with rutting sign. Scrapes and rubs were everywhere,

During the rut, bucks can often be called into range with grunt tubes. Realize, however, that rut activity will change each year because of lunar influences, which might cause variances in buck rutting behavior year to year.

During the pre-rut, white-tailed bucks conserve energy by bedding for long periods of time. They'll need this energy once rut activity kicks into high gear. Wayne Laroche and I disagree with traditional thinking that puts peak rutting activity near mid-November every year.

When Wayne Laroche heard Maine's peak breeding in deer always occurred Nov. 15, his years as a fisheries researcher told him something was amiss.

and the rutting behavior he saw caused him to make plans to hunt the same week the next year.

When November 1992 rolled around, he headed back to Maine's North Woods, hoping for a repeat of 1991. It didn't happen. The woods were dead and he found little rutting sign the first week of November. Why? In '92, the rutting moon occurred Nov. 9, a full 17 days later than it did in 1991. I believe rutting activity didn't kick into high gear until after Laroche was done hunting in '92.

When he returned from that hunt, Laroche contacted Maine's Department of Natural Resources and asked for rutting information. He was told peak breeding always occurs Nov. 15. His years as a fisheries researcher told him something was amiss. Knowing how moonlight affected fish, he wondered if it could also affect whitetails. As 1992 flowed into 1993, he began searching for answers.

Too Many Coincidences

As Laroche questioned the traditional acceptance of peak breeding dates in Northern whitetails, he looked at other factors that might cause rutting behavior to change each year. The more he dug, the more closely he looked at the moon's possible influences. When too many coincidences occur in nature, they usually suggest some causal relationships. Laroche concluded there were simply too many coincidences associating lunar conditions with the whitetail's reproductive cycle.

The widely accepted belief is that peak breeding north of the Mason-Dixon Line (Pennsylvania/Maryland border) occurs about Nov. 15 each year, and is set by photoperiod.

Laroche and I no longer believe that. After several observations of early-November rutting behavior in Vermont and Maine, Laroche concluded that rut activity was often insignificant by mid-November. He found the timing of peak rutting activity could vary each year by as much as three weeks. Could the moon cause such swings?

Let's look at the facts and coincidences Laroche studied before forming his hypothesis.

○ The moon's lunar cycle is 29½ days. A white-tailed doe's estrus cycle is

This buck is Flehmening, or lip-curling, to test if a nearby doe is in estrus. Bucks will typically increase their home range from about 1,000 acres to more than 4,000 acres once they're on the prowl for a receptive doe. Wayne Laroche and I believe the full (rutting) moon in late October or November triggers the doe's estrous cycle and increases rutting behavior by bucks.

28 to 29 days (Halls & House, 1984). A coincidence?

○ The deer's pineal gland is capable of responding to light by producing hormones that affect and regulate the reproductive cycle. Could the moon provide this light source?

○ The whitetail's eyes are adapted for nocturnal activity, having more rods than cones. Rods are 100 times more sensitive to light than cones. However, they don't detect color and have poorer resolution than cones. Because of this, deer's eyes are more sensitive to moonlight than are human eyes. Is there a reason for that?

○ A white-tailed doe's average gestation period is 199 days (Halls & House, 1984). Because most does are bred under a dark-moon period, Laroche calculated the moon phase that occurs 199 days after most does are bred. It worked out to be within a day of a third-quarter moon phase. He believes it might not be coincidental. Indeed, it might be possible that by being born under a darker moon, fawns are more likely to escape predation.

○ In the Northern hemisphere, the brightest full moons and the most moonlight delivered per lunar cycle occur in October, November, December and January, and November and December produce the brightest moonlight. Could that trigger a doe's estrous cycle and a buck's rutting behavior?

○ Progesterone levels drop and estrogen levels rise rapidly in does beginning seven days before estrus. The date of the third-quarter lunar phase (waning moon) that marks the beginning of the dark cycle is seven days before the new moon.

○ Hormone levels change in urine as they change in blood. Bucks, with their highly sensitive olfactory organs, detect these changes through Flehmening, or lip-curling. This behavior is nothing more than a visual sign of a buck performing a chemical test to see if a doe is in estrus. Could the moon's phases trigger this buck behavior? Could the late October or November full moon trigger other behaviors, such as chasing and breeding?

These coincidences made Laroche look long and hard at the moon's possible effect on whitetails. By the time he and I began talking in 1994-95, Laroche was well on his way to uncovering interesting information. In our early conversations, I learned how he was using computer models, light meters and astronomical data to develop his ideas. After much thought and some data from me, he formed the following hypothesis on how the moon affects rut-related deer behavior:

Laroche's Hypothesis

At some point in autumn, the amount of sunlight decreases enough to reset the whitetail's reproductive clock, thus placing the breeding season in

Research that Wayne Laroche and I are conducting has found that 70 percent to 80 percent of adult does will be bred after the rutting moon. We don't think that high percentage is just an unexplained, repetitive coincidence.

November, December and January in the Northern hemisphere. Once the doe's reproductive cycle is reset by a specific amount of sunlight, her estrous cycle is ready to be cued by moonlight, which provides a bright light stimulus to the pineal gland several nights in a row each lunar month. Then, the rapid decrease in lunar brightness during the moon's third quarter triggers hormonal production by the pineal gland. Physiological changes prompted by the pineal gland culminate in ovulation and estrus.

A Northern doe's estrogen level peaks around Nov. 1 as does a buck's sperm count. With both sexes poised to breed, it stands to reason a mechanism must be in place if the doe is to enter estrus and be bred under the darker phases of the moon, which is the third quarter to first quarter. That mechanism in the North is the second full moon after the autumnal equinox, which I call the rutting moon. (Note: See Chapter 16, where I discuss two deviations to this cycle.)

The "Rut Predictor Chart"

After much analysis, Laroche was convinced the full (rutting) moon in late October or November was profoundly influencing the rutting and

In 1997, Wayne Laroche developed a chart to predict daily whitetail activity in the fall. Starting in 1999, Laroche's chart was incorporated into **Deer & Deer Hunting** *magazine's annual calendar.*

breeding behavior of Northern whitetails. Between his computer programs and my actual breeding data, Laroche felt confident he had the information to produce a tool for deer hunters.

In 1997 he introduced his "Rut Predictor Chart." The accompanying photo shows the whitetail characters he uses to show which deer behavior to expect each day of autumn and early winter. These characters represent resting (bedding), feeding, seeking, chasing and tending (breeding).

In 1999, *Deer & Deer Hunting* magazine began incorporating Laroche's "Rut Predictor Chart" in its popular annual "Whitetail Calendar." The beauty of this visual aid is that hunters can look at each month of the hunting season to find the moon phase and daily deer behavior to expect. In addition, the characters are shown in different colors to represent Northern and Southern behavior.

In Chapter 5, I'll outline my part in assisting Laroche, and share my insights into how the rutting moon affects the rut's timing.

CHAPTER 5

Breaking Through: Charlie Alsheimer's Research

Have you ever had a gut feeling you were right about something or that you were on to something but couldn't quite put your finger on it?

That's where I was in 1994 regarding this moon thing. I realized at the time I was close to figuring out how the rutting moon related to the rut's timing, but I couldn't seem to connect the dots.

My frustration ended when I met Wayne Laroche. Our discussion about the moon's effect on the rut was actually a spin-off during an interview in which I was asking how he developed his Trackometer device. (This caliber-like device measures deer tracks to estimate the deer's live and dressed weights.) Before long, we were sharing our findings about the moon's influence on whitetails. After several in-depth conversations, I began to see the light.

Flawed Research?

I admire and deeply respect the many things deer researchers have done over the years. Without that research, the white-tailed deer likely wouldn't have thrived the way it has. However, at risk of being attacked by professional biologists, I'll stick my neck out and say some research is not as accurate as I would like.

Two examples are fetus-aging estimates and aging deer through tooth wear. My thoughts regarding these methods result from 20 years of full-time work in the field. Also, during the past eight years I've owned whitetails and been part of three research projects. That doesn't make me an expert, but the longer I work with deer, the more things seem to vary.

For example, I've seen problems arise when biologists try to prove a point using fetus and tooth-wear aging. Anyone who spends time around deer has seen someone ask a biologist a deer's age. The biologist looks at the jawbone briefly and confidently states a specific age like 3½ or 4½ years old. The person asking the question takes this as

This is my best white-tailed buck in more than 40 years of hunting. I killed him during the peak of the breeding phase as he cruised through the woods in early afternoon. My experience in the woods as a deer hunter and photographer sometimes causes me to question certain assumptions and specifics of certain deer research from the past 50 years.

The only precise way to age a deer is to have a tooth cross-sectioned and examined under a microscope. Biologists should ensure hunters understand tooth-wear aging is an estimate for mature deer, not an absolute.

gospel. In reality, after a deer passes 2½ years of age, the tooth-wear/replacement method for aging deer is only an intelligent estimate, not a precise fact.

A benefit of working with confined deer is that you know their exact age. To prove my point, I sometimes hand a known-age jawbone to a biologist and ask him to estimate the deer's age. The biologists typically come close, but more times than not they're off by one to three years.

I realize many factors go into tooth-wear aging, but I wonder about a system when biologists too often say a specific jaw is "without question" from a 3½-, 4½- or 5½-year-old deer. While tooth-wear aging provides an estimate, the only precise way to age a deer is to have the tooth cross-sectioned and examined under a microscope. Biologists should make sure hunters understand that tooth-wear aging is strictly a ballpark estimate for mature deer, not an absolute.

The same goes for fetus-aging techniques. Fetus aging and the fetus scale are wonderful tools that can aid biologists, but the bottom line is that fetus aging, like jawbone aging, only gets you in the ballpark. Basically, the fetus-aging process chronicles various physical developments during the 181- to 200-day gestation process. Some fetuses reach maturity at 181 days while others take up to 200 days. Many factors account for this, but there is a disparity of nearly 20 days.

I note this because nearly all research on deer breeding in Northern whitetails is based on fetal development. Research by New York's L.W. Jackson and W.T. Hesselton on Northern breeding dates for whitetails used the fetuses from dog- and road-killed does to determine conception dates. The 20-day "fudge factor" dramatically throws off the estimated conception date.

Better Data

Because the fetus-aging technique is not exact, Laroche and I have tried to find more accurate data collection. Our research data comes from live animals instead of dead ones. When we began our moon

During the rut it's not uncommon for a subordinate buck to travel with a mature buck. When looking at the teeth of deer in different age classes, it's easier and more accurate to judge the age of deer 2½ years old and younger than it is to estimate the age of mature deer using the tooth-wear dating method.

Yearling does — which are 1.5 years old — are irregular when they breed the first time. Some of them conceive after the pre-rut moon and some don't conceive until the post-rut moon period.

study, we only had six Northern does I could accurately monitor. Laroche said we should locate at least 30 does we could track each year to get the day they conceived and the day they gave birth.

We now have about 50 does in our research project. All of the does (except for one location) are north of the 35th latitude, with most at or near the 40th latitude. The most important factor in our work is that I now know the exact day most of these does are bred and, in some cases, the exact hour. I also know if they "took" the first time or required a second cycle to conceive.

It's not uncommon for 10 percent to 20 percent of adult does to fail to conceive the first time they're bred. I've also found the yearling does — which are 1½ years old — are irregular when they breed the first time. Some of them conceive after the pre-rut moon and some don't conceive until after the post-rut moon period. Mature does (2½ years or older) are predictable, providing they're healthy.

I'm finding that nearly 80 percent of the mature does in our project are bred during or very close to the 14-day window Laroche and I predicted the past several years. What follows is an example of how I collect my data.

Four Girls, Four Years

Let's look at four of my research does: Buttercup, Carla, Daisy and Janelle. As I write this chapter, these does are 9, 5, 3 and 2 years old, respectively.

Buttercup was born in the heart of New York's Adirondack Mountains. Carla was born on a breeding operation in Steuben County, N.Y. I bought Buttercup and Carla, and moved them to my facility in October 1995. Daisy is Buttercup's daughter and was the first fawn born in my facility. Janelle is Carla's daughter and was also born here.

All the does are healthy, although Buttercup is aging a bit. Nutritionally, all the deer have lush food plots and ample mast for food. In addition, they're fed a daily 17.5 percent protein mix with all

Data I've been collecting from dozens of does substantiates the breeding dates Wayne Laroche and I have been predicting for several years. We started off with six does in our sample group, but expanded it to about 50 by 1999.

the minerals and vitamins they need. In winter I increase the carbohydrates they require during this time. So, they have everything that's required, and then some, for a balanced diet.

In 1995, the rutting moon was Nov. 7. When the rutting moon occurs during the first week of November, I consider this to be a classic or traditional rut. That is, breeding takes place from mid- to late November in the North — the rutting time-line I had been taught. The only two does in my facility in 1995 were Carla and Buttercup. Carla was bred Nov. 17 and Buttercup Nov. 21, dates that fell within the predicted breeding window. On June 6, 1996, Buttercup gave birth to Daisy.

In 1996 the rutting moon showed up early and shined full Oct. 26. Buttercup bred Nov. 1 and Carla bred Nov. 4, again, right in the breeding window Laroche and I had predicted for most Northern does. However, Buttercup didn't take when she was bred, and cycled a second time. She bred again Thanksgiving Day, Nov. 28. By that time Daisy was nearly 6 months old and she was a large fawn. On

Just before the rut's breeding phase, rattling can be an excellent way to lure a big buck into range. Peak rutting activity will vary each year, depending on the timing of the rutting moon. When this full moon occurs the first week of November, it sets the stage for a "traditional" rut, which means peak breeding will occur in mid- to late November.

Dec. 2, the bucks began paying close attention to her. For the next two days I saw some chasing but no breeding. Was she ever bred? I don't know. However, she bore no fawns in Spring 1997.

In 1997, the rutting moon came late: Nov. 14. This time Carla was bred first — Nov. 19. Buttercup followed Nov. 21. Daisy was now 1½ years old, and she was a bit unpredictable. She bred Nov. 13, didn't take, and was bred again Dec. 12, 29 days later. The mature does again fell into the breeding window Laroche and I had predicted. We saw the pattern forming.

In 1998, the rutting moon was once again what I call a traditional

By watching when the rutting moon will occur, it's relatively easy to predict the 14-day breeding period that will soon follow. Wayne Laroche and I have been able to accurately predict this window of opportunity the past several years, and breeding by our research does has corroborated our predictions.

Once the breeding phase is over, killing a buck like this is a real challenge.
The rut quickly drains the fat and energy reserves of even the healthiest bucks.

rutting moon, falling Nov 4. Carla started things off when she was bred Nov. 13, right on schedule. Daisy, now a mature doe, was bred Nov. 17, within the breeding window. Buttercup kept things consistent, and was bred Nov. 21. My last doe, Janelle (Carla's daughter) was now an unpredictable 1½-year-old. She fell through the cracks a little, and was bred Nov. 30. She was off a little, but not by much.

More Than a Coincidence

That information is just some of the data I'm collecting at my facility. True, it's under controlled conditions, but nothing was or will be done to manipulate the situation. No drugs or anything artificial were used to alter the does' estrous cycles at different times each year. None of the conditions were created by man.

Furthermore, there is much more to the process I described above. As I said, we have many more deer in the project. My point is that the data I'm collecting from other locations closely resembles what I'm seeing at my facility.

When I first asked certain deer breeders for their help, many, but

During the breeding phase, if a buck is locked up on a doe, the doe will dictate his every move. Unless the doe goes on the move, you'll probably never see the buck that is tending her.

not all, were skeptical. Like me, they had bought into the notion that mid- to late-November breeding was the annual deal, so they never gave different ideas much thought. However, when the breeders began collecting data for me, I received all kinds of positive comments regarding what I was doing. I've even received phone calls from a deer breeder in Missouri commenting and asking: "You sure nailed it last year. How in the world did you ever get on to this?" Needless to say, the whole process has been enlightening, not to mention exciting.

Where Do I Go from Here?

I see no need to stop doing what Laroche and I started in 1994. It's too much fun, especially now that the data collection system is in place. The goal is to put together 15 years of hard data using live deer, so that the rutting moon concept can be looked at over a long time period.

With each passing year, things become more firm. There is no question in my mind that the rutting moon has a significant influence on the North's rut, and that includes everything from rubbing to scraping to fighting to chasing to breeding.

The combination of all of these things is what gives the hunter an advantage during those magical days.

CHAPTER 6

The Whitetail's Autumn Behavior

Have you ever sat on a stand and tried analyzing the whitetail's autumn behavior? Have you ever wondered when the pre-rut, rut, and post-rut begin and end, or which aspect of the rut is most fascinating?

When I began deer hunting, I didn't know much about the whitetail's rutting behavior. During my youth, I viewed the rut as one frenzied two-week period in the whitetail's life. After 30 years of extensively hunting and photographing whitetails, I now realize the rut's chemistry is more complex than I originally thought.

Understanding whitetails during autumn, especially as it relates to the rut, requires knowledge of deer behavior and what triggers the rut's various phases. Everything that precedes breeding — velvet peeling, rubbing, scraping, chasing and fighting — has a purpose. No aspect of the rut is an isolated occurrence. All the activities blend to create one of nature's most incredible spectacles.

The Preparation

Photoperiodism — the behavioral and physiological responses to changing amounts of daylight — drives nature's timetable, from leaves growing on trees to antlers growing on deer. Though summer's growing season is leisurely for whitetails, subtle changes within the buck population shape a herd's pecking order for fall. Dominant bucks engage in stare-downs, shadowing and, in some cases, flailing with their hoofs. These behaviors help determine which buck could become the bull of the woods when the breeding game begins.

Nature does not load bucks with their full arsenal before the precise time each weapon is needed. Can you imagine what the woods would be like if a buck's testosterone level peaked in early September rather than early November?

By late August, bucks' velvet dries, cracks and peels. About the same time, just enough testosterone surges through their system to inspire rubbing. Then, near the end of September, the testosterone "valve" opens wider, stimulating scraping.

By mid-October, with the days cooler and testosterone levels

As summer ends, velvet-clad bucks increase their scraping frequency. I believe scraping is a satisfying, conditioned response for bucks. When working an overhanging licking branch, a buck is greatly satisfied by the branch massaging its forehead, preorbital and nasal glands.

In September, bucks are still in bachelor groups, but these associations are pretty much broken up by the time the pre-rut moon arrives. As testosterone levels increase in bucks, their tolerance for each other decreases.

higher, bucks move more during daylight. Does' estrogen levels climb, and they begin smelling differently. By early November, bucks' testosterone levels and does' estrogen levels have peaked, setting the stage for what deer hunters call "the rut."

The Rut's Confusing Terms

When someone mentions pre-rut, rut or post-rut to me, I always ask them to define what those terms mean to them so I can best answer their question. Those terms have been used so many ways the past 50 years that it's difficult to define them universally.

For biologists and researchers, pre-rut usually defines all behaviors that occur before full-blown breeding. In contrast, most hunters think of the pre-rut as the early autumn period when days are warm and little rubbing, scraping or fighting occurs.

To researchers, the word "rut" usually means the actual breeding period. But most hunters think it means that much and more, namely the time bucks are going bonkers while rubbing, scraping, chasing and fighting.

Once their antler velvet peels, bucks will begin to spar with each other. Such encounters can last from one to 30 minutes, depending on the attitude of the participants. Sparring helps the bucks determine their place in the herd's male pecking order.

During the rut's seeking and chasing phases, mature bucks in search of does will often make six to 12 scrapes per hour. They seldom rest as they cruise the woods desperately seeking a receptive doe.

Hunters and biologists agree the post-rut is the period and behavior associated with the time after breeding ends. So, the mere study and use of these words can be confusing. Though I believe pre-rut, rut and post-rut are good ways to describe a whitetail's autumn behavior, I break it down more precisely.

The Dominance Phase

Dominance among white-tailed deer is progressive and ever-changing. Once a buck's velvet peels, it begins the physical training for its greatest game — breeding. In many ways, this period reminds me of an athlete's preseason training regimen. A buck is fat-laden as summer ends, far different from what it will be by Oct. 1. Once its antlers are hard, a buck begins to rub more frequently as daylight continually shortens. A buck rubs frequently for two obvious reasons. First, like a boxer working a speed bag, a buck rubbing a tree is strengthening its neck and shoulder muscles. Second, rubbing allows a buck to leave its scent and visual markers so other deer know it has

It takes a big, mature buck to make a rub like this. As the rut progresses, rubs like this will become more common if there are mature bucks in the area.

In addition to working a scrape's overhanging licking branch, a buck will paw the ground free of debris before urinating under the branch. It's my belief that scrapes are almost exclusively the domain of bucks. In all my years of hunting and photographing, I've seen does interact at scrapes less than 20 times.

been there and will return when breeding begins.

With ever-increasing testosterone in its system, a buck adds another dimension to its identity by making scrapes. Scraping, like rubbing, allows a buck to make its presence known by dispensing scent throughout its area.

Hunters debate whether scraping is primarily a "buck thing" or if it's done to attract does. In more than 30 years of photographing and hunting deer from Texas to Canada, I've seen less than 20 does interact at scrapes. During this time I've seen and photographed hundreds of bucks making scrapes. So, based on this, it's my view that scraping is a buck behavior; in this case a way to show its dominance.

An encounter between two mature bucks of equal size will erupt into a fight if one of the antagonists doesn't back down to common intimidation tactics. Shadowing or stare-downs like this one will usually persuade one of the bucks to back away and move on.

I believe scraping is also a satisfying, conditioned response for bucks. When working an overhanging licking branch, a buck is greatly satisfied by the branch massaging its forehead, preorbital and nasal glands. I don't believe a buck consciously knows it is spreading its scent to other deer.

Judging by the hundreds of photos I've taken of scraping bucks, it appears the satisfying and stimulating aspects of scraping might largely explain why a buck performs the behaviors frequently. I'm not saying scent-depositing isn't a big part of scraping, because it is. But I'm convinced the dynamics of scraping are incredibly complex and serve several functions, probably more than we'll ever realize.

Physical Competition

With rubbing and scraping comes physical competition. Once free of velvet, most bucks begin sparring. This is a way to exercise while

Vicious fights like this one usually last less than five minutes. On rare occasions, bucks will lock antlers and be unable to break away from each other. When that happens, the combatants usually pay with their lives.

testing the herd's competitive waters. For the most part, sparring matches are playful skirmishes between two bucks of equal size and stature. However, on occasion, sparring can get out of hand and become ugly. The best analogy I can offer is two teen-age brothers playfully wrestling on the living-room floor. Before they realize it, one gets his nose bloodied and tempers flare. While photographing in fall, I've often seen sparring contests between bucks follow a similar sequence.

As breeding time nears, bucks become adventurous, and trouble often befalls a traveling buck. A buck's range often expands from about 600 acres in summer to 4,000 or more acres by early November. A whitetail's summer and early-fall pecking order falls apart, because strange bucks continually trespass on each other's turf. Chaos invades the whitetail's world!

The Seeking Phase

Bucks are more vocal in autumn than at any other time of the year. By November, bucks communicate with other deer by emitting

When the rut becomes full-blown, bucks will lip-curl — also known as Flehmening — wherever they find doe urine. This allows them to test whether the doe is in estrus and possibly ready to breed.

A doe will smell "right" for about 72 hours when she is in estrus, but she will only allow the buck to breed her during the 24-hour period in which she can be impregnated. Even so, a buck will constantly hound the doe during the entire three-day period.

grunts, bleats, snorts and snort-wheezes.

With maximum levels of testosterone now flowing, bucks look feverishly for an estrous doe. Their noses dictate when and where bucks go. No doe group is safe as bucks weave across their expanded territory. At this time, all the dynamics of buck behavior unite. Bucks are now finely tuned physical specimens that spend every waking hour rubbing, scraping and looking for does. Judging by research I've conducted for several years, an active buck might make six to 12 scrapes per hour during this rut phase. The frequency depends on how sexually active a given buck is.

At this time, bucks also lip-curl — a behavior scientists call "Flehmening" — far more than in previous months. They exhibit this behavior when they find a place where a doe has urinated.

Lip-curling allows a buck to learn if a doe is entering estrus. The buck traps scent from a doe's urine in its nose and mouth, and then lip-curls. This helps the buck's scent-analyzing device — the vomero-nasal organ in the roof of its mouth — pinpoint the doe's status.

How many times will a buck breed an estrous doe? I once photographed a buck breed a doe five times during a seven-hour span. If she doesn't "take," she will re-cycle into estrus 28 days later and try again to get pregnant.

When a mature buck or an aggressive yearling buck encounters a stranger or a recognized contender, one or two things usually occur. Stare-downs or shadowing usually occur first. It's generally a buck's antlers and body size that cause one antagonist to cut short the encounter by shying away. Most bucks are aware of the size of their antlers and body, and can quickly size up the situation. However, if two bucks of similar size — with testosterone-injected attitudes to match — find each other, the results can get ugly.

If a fight to the death begins, the scene can be spectacular. Antlers become ice picks, and there are no rules of fair fighting. A buck's objective is to knock his opponent to the ground, and then stick his antlers into his opponent's abdomen or hindquarters. Such fights can be gruesome, and when it's over, victor and loser alike often need time to recover before resuming their pursuit of does. Combatants even die from their wounds.

During the chase phase, a buck will chase every doe it encounters. Such meetings often resemble a cutting horse trying to cut a calf out of a herd of cows. A buck can be persistent as it tries to find a doe that won't run.

Of all the times to hunt, the seeking phase is one of the best, especially for a tree-stand hunter. The peak of this period is usually three to four days before and two to three days after the rutting moon. During this time, bucks are on the move but not yet chasing every doe they encounter. Their movement patterns through funnels and along scrape and rub lines are more predictable. Unfortunately, the seeking phase only lasts a short time before blending into the chase phase.

The Chase Phase

The chase phase often gets confused with the seeking phase. The two behavior periods overlap, but they're different. This phase usually begins a couple days after the rutting moon and lasts three to four days into the full blown breeding phase. During the chase phase, does are almost entering estrus, and bucks are frantically trying to be the first to find them. Now a buck will chase every doe it encounters. Such meetings often resemble a cutting horse trying to cut a calf out of a herd of cows. A buck can be persistent, knowing it will eventually find a doe that won't run. During the chase phase, scraping and rubbing continue, and in many cases can be intense, especially in a well-tuned herd. The chase phase often brings more intense fights, especially if two bucks pursue the same doe.

The chase phase can be a great time to hunt, but it often gets frustrating because the action can take bucks out of range as they chase does.

Tending and Breeding Phase

This is the stage that gives the rut its name. When a doe finally enters estrus, it will accept a buck's company wherever it goes. In many parts of North America, the doe-to-buck ratios are so weighted toward females that all available bucks can easily find a hot doe. When breeding begins, scraping nearly ceases and bucks curtail much of the activity that took place throughout the rut's dominance, seeking and chasing phases.

Dominant breeder bucks never rest as they try to run off intruder bucks. Because they have no time to rest or eat, breeder bucks can lose up to 25 percent of their weight during the rut's seeking, chasing and breeding phases.

This phase usually begins five to seven days after the rutting moon and lasts about 14 days. During this time, 70 percent to 80 percent of mature does will be bred.

Rather than traveling, a buck will stay with a hot doe for up to 72 hours. For the first 24 hours, a doe will smell right, but won't be ready to breed. During the second 24 hours, the doe will be in full estrus and allow the buck to breed her several times. Then, because she continues to smell right for the last 24 hours, a buck will continue to stay with her.

During those three days, a buck will move only when the doe moves. Because most does cover little ground, deer activity can seemingly halt during this time. Only when the doe cycles out of estrus will the buck move on to look for another estrous doe.

The first does to come into estrus will often cause a commotion by attracting several bucks. When that happens, a dominant breeder buck never rests as he tries to run off all intruder bucks in order to stay in position to breed the doe. Because they have no time to rest or eat, breeder bucks can lose up to 25 percent of their weight during the rut's seeking, chasing and breeding phases.

Of all the rut's phases, the breeding time can be the most difficult to hunt because movement is limited. At this time, about the only way tree-stand hunters will see action is to place their stands in the hot doe's core area or sites frequented by doe groups.

Post-Rut: The Recovery Time

By the time a whitetail's prime breeding period ends, a buck's testosterone level is plummeting. A breeder buck is also so rut-worn that its body is in a near melt-down. Researchers have found that some bucks are so worn down by the time breeding is over that they'll have trouble surviving a hard winter. With less testosterone to drive them, bucks go into a resting and feeding mode as soon as the November breeding ceases. In regions with high doe-to-buck ratios, the stress of an extended breeding season decreases the survival chances of many breeder bucks.

Even with does entering estrus at nontraditional times, such as December and January, the rutting behavior of bucks will not be as intense as it was earlier. Limited, subdued chasing will occur, but scraping and serious fighting is mostly over. Most post-rut behavior is done by subordinate bucks in the form of sparring, but minor scraping and rubbing will likely occur.

Survival again becomes more important than breeding. The post-rut is a time for bucks to restore fat and energy reserves. The bucks seem to know their only chance of surviving a Northern winter is to rest and feed heavily.

Conclusion

The whitetail's rut is an amazing and complex phenomenon. It's made up of an array of behavioral traits, each distinctly different but interwoven. Each rut phase works in concert with the others to ensure the species' survival.

In the next four chapters I'll share how I hunt the various phases of the pre-rut, rutting and post-rut moons.

THE RUT'S TIMING IS EVERYTHING

CHAPTER 7

The Rut's Timing is Everything

The day was Nov. 19, 1997, five days after the full moon. It was the third day of New York's shotgun season, and business had kept me from hunting earlier in the day. With three hours of daylight left, I headed to one of my favorite stands on our farm.

For nearly 300 yards, I crept through thick hardwoods and hemlocks. The day was clear and cold, and a foot of powder snow made for quiet walking. When I was within 100 yards of my tree stand, I slowed to a snail's pace. The woods were dead calm and I didn't want to ruin the evening's hunt by spooking deer. After reaching my tree, I took great pains to climb silently into the stand. Once on the permanent stand's platform, I rested my shotgun against the tree before scanning the woods in every direction.

Eye Catcher

Behind the stand and up a steep bank, a brown spot caught my eye. I had hunted here the night before and passed up a 4-pointer. I didn't recall seeing the dark spot in the snow and low hemlock growth. I fished my binoculars out of my hunting coat. I couldn't believe what I was looking at 60 yards away. A big buck was bedded, angling away. Only his hindquarters were in clear view. His ribs, front shoulders and head were obscured by thick saplings. All around him was thick brush and hemlocks. I'm sure he felt secure bedded in such tight quarters. Even so, I couldn't believe I had been able to climb into the stand undetected. For the next 45 minutes the buck and I played out the greatest drama I've encountered in the deer woods.

Because of my seat's location and where the buck was lying, I couldn't sit down and shoot. I had to stand to keep an eye on him. From years of photographing bedded whitetails, I knew of just two ways the buck would get up: He would bolt out of his bed and run, or he would stand and stretch before taking a step. Therefore, I kept the scope on him at all times. I didn't want to risk not being able to react fast enough if he

At left, this is the buck I describe in the beginning of this chapter. Believe it or not, a flock of wild turkeys unwittingly urged the buck into my cross-hairs after a 45-minute standoff.

Being in the woods during the rut's chase phase increases your chances greatly. Bucks can act like race horses bursting out of the gate at the Kentucky Derby. For several days they rush around the woods releasing pent up energy.

jumped up and ran.

Even if he did get up, I wasn't sure I could get a shot because of the thick brush. Through my 7X scope I studied the saplings in front of him to see if I could find a shooting lane. It looked like I would have about a 6-inch opening if he stepped into it. If he moved in any other direction I wouldn't have a shot.

Study Time

I studied the buck for the next 15 minutes. His eyes were fixed on the hemlocks in front of his nose. This made me think a doe might be bedded in front of him, although I couldn't see anything. Despite resting the gun against a tree, my arm tired after the first 20 minutes and I had to bring it down to rest. About that time I realized I would have to take the initiative. Because the day was ending fast, if I didn't try to get him up, it would quickly be "O-dark-30."

With my shotgun shouldered and braced against the tree, I got out the grunt tube and blew softly. He didn't hear me. I gave two loud guttural

When the rutting moon shines full, the stage is set for the rut to explode. If it occurs the first eight days of November, you might witness a classic rut — the kind most hunters envision when they think of a frenzied rut.

grunts and the buck looked my way. I thought he would get up but he didn't. Instead, he looked back into the hemlocks. His behavior indicated a doe was with him, and I knew he wouldn't leave her for anything.

Forty minutes into the ordeal, the buck began to doze, resting his muzzle in the snow. While I contemplated my next move, I got a break. A flock of turkeys was moving off an oak flat atop the steep slope above him, heading for a roost. With my scope on the buck, I saw two long-beards walking straight at him. When one of the gobblers was 10 yards from the buck, I could see he was going to get up. I clicked the safety off and got ready. He stood, stretched and stepped into the narrow opening.

Nearly every good licking branch gets worked in a buck's core area during the rut's seeking and chase phases. Once breeding becomes prevalent, however, an air of calm starts to return to the woods.

When mature bucks expand their range in their quest for a receptive doe, they encounter bucks they've never seen before. Fights become inevitable.

At the roar of the 12-gauge, the hard-hit buck lunged forward and the woods exploded. Turkeys flew everywhere and a doe ran through my scope picture. She stopped after about 20 yards and a second deer, a yearling 4-pointer, rose from his bed in the hemlocks. He walked up to the doe, licked her flanks, and bred her on the hillside within sight of me and the big buck I had just killed. I couldn't believe the scene.

In more than 40 years in the deer woods, I had never encountered anything like that 45-minute drama.

Timing the Moon and the Rut

I shared that 1997 hunting experience for two reasons. First, it points out how the rut makes a white-tailed buck more vulnerable. Second, and most importantly, it shows how predictable the rut can be when the rutting moon period is factored in. That's what this book is all about.

In 1997, the rutting moon was Nov. 14. I made the following prediction in the September 1997 issue of *Deer & Deer Hunting*: "If past patterns hold true this year, the first week of November doesn't look promising. However, my records show if the weather cooperates —

During the rut's chase phase, bucks are so focused on finding a hot doe that they let their guard down and become more vulnerable to patient hunters.

It's critical to know when the rut kicks in so you can take advantage of the best time to be in the woods. Scraping and chasing are at a fever pitch for about 10 days before breeding begins, which greatly increases your chances.

meaning cool temperatures with a least some clear skies — and hunting pressure isn't high, buck activity should become very good around Nov. 11 or 12, just before the full moon. From Nov. 11 until the prime breeding begins around Nov. 20 and 21, bucks should be highly active if the region you hunt has a reasonable doe-to-buck ratio."

Anytime I stick my neck out with a prediction, part of me says, "Alsheimer, do you really want to do this?" Even though I believe more strongly each year in what Laroche and I are doing, the feeling is always there, though it is waning. Well, 1997 is history. The data collected in Fall 1997 and Spring '98 shows that more than 70 percent of the does in the research project were bred in or near the peak Nov. 20 to 27 window we had predicted.

They say repetition is the key to learning, so to better understand how the rutting moon affects the rut's timing, allow me to repeat how it works. Roughly five to seven days after the rutting moon, does begin coming into estrus. The full-blown 14-day breeding window follows. That means a number of things for hunters.

For starters, it's critical to know when the rut kicks in so you can take advantage of the best window of opportunity the rut can offer. Second, knowing that scraping and chasing are at a fever pitch for about 10 days just before breeding begins can greatly increase your chances. Third, it's important to know when scraping and other rutting behaviors start tapering off so you can anticipate shifts in hunting strategy.

At risk of sounding repetitive, many factors influence the rut's timing, but all things being equal, daytime activity normally picks up three to four days before the rutting moon shines full. To our eye, the moon appears full or nearly full two days before its full phase. I believe whitetailed bucks sense something significant is occurring in the doe population, and start becoming active on the eve of the rutting moon.

And They're Off!

I believe this "sense" has much to do with the amount of sex-related pheromones hovering in the air. The way bucks respond to these scents

During the rut, several bucks will work the same scrape, especially if the scrape is in a prime travel corridor.

In a well-tuned herd that has a relatively balanced sex ratio, a mature buck can breed about 10 does. When herd sex ratios are skewed heavily toward does, the breeding period is extended and bucks do more breeding. Stress can take a heavy toll, especially on older bucks.

reminds me of race horses at the Kentucky Derby's starting gate. When those horses burst from the gates, they hit the track with a lot of pent up energy. It's only much later that they get the spoils, in this case the finish line. In between, they expend a tremendous amount of energy.

The same holds true for white-tailed bucks. With the smell of does everywhere, bucks jump out of the gates a couple of days before the rutting moon shines full. If temperatures are cool and human pressure is minimal, they go ballistic for the next 10 days. During the early part of the race, bucks can stay on their hoofs for six hours at a clip and make six to 12 scrapes per hour. Such behavior can only be called chaos. But be warned: The chaos can end as quickly as it began, especially if the doe-to-buck ratios exceed 4-1. Bonker bucks become breeding bucks in a heartbeat once does are in estrus. When that happens, things get significantly calmer in the woods.

Classifying the Rut

After six years of intense study, I believe the intensity of each year's

Hunting over active scrapes can offer incredible opportunities during the rut. Once breeding begins, however, scrapes go "silent" and hunters who doggedly stake out dormant scrapes are seldom rewarded.

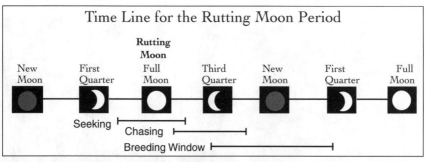

My research with Wayne Laroche has found that 70 percent to 80 percent of adult does will breed during the "breeding window."

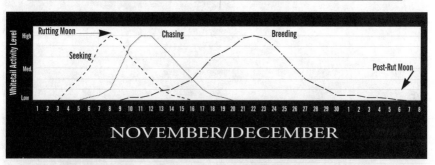

These charts show how rutting activity typically unfolds during a classic November rut. I define a classic rut as one that occurs Nov. 1-8. It's important to note that the seeking, chasing and tending lines do not work independently of each other. Rather, they work together and should be viewed as one blending into the next as the rut progresses.

rut is a little different because of when the rutting moon occurs. From journals and observations I've made since beginning my study in 1993, we'll see a classic rut if the rutting moon occurs during the first eight days in November. I define a classic rut as one that resembles what most hunters envision the rut to be. For example, hunters in my region have long preached the best time to hunt deer in New York's Adirondack Mountains is always around Nov. 11. If you look at much of the old writings, you'll find hunters used to think the best time to be on the trail of a rut-crazed buck was Nov. 10 to 15. Also, most of the older breeding research said peak whitetail breeding occurs Nov. 15 to 30 in the North.

I believe the rut is most intense when the rutting moon occurs the first eight days of November. This belief stems from my years of observations, accurate breeding data, and the fact white-tailed bucks and does reach their hormonal peak around Nov. 1. When cool temperatures, the rutting moon and the deer's hormonal peak occur in unison, the rut can

If you find rubs like this in prime scraping locations, the chances for shooting a mature buck are excellent.

be explosive. That mix shapes people's opinions about when the rut occurs. But ruts like that only occur about once every three years.

When the rutting moon does not occur the first eight days of November, at least two factors in the previous paragraph — moon and hormone peak — are not synchronized. And if warm temperatures settle in during the rutting moon, all three factors can be out of sync. That scenario can make things tough in the deer woods.

The data I've collected so far makes me think the chase phase is less intense when the rutting moon occurs outside the Nov. 1 to 8 window.

Timing Recap

Although there are parallels between the pre-rut, rutting and post-rut moons, each is significantly different. It's important to keep your eye on the calendar so you'll know what to expect.

In the case of the pre-rut moon, deer activity will be sporadic during this full-moon period. There will certainly be a little chasing, scraping

About the time the rutting moon arrives, a buck has a fire in his belly and he's ready to go. Starting a few days before and ending about 10 days after the rutting moon, the woods will be humming with deer activity.

and breeding. It's just too early for bucks to be wound up and on the go like they'll be 30 days later.

About the time the rutting moon arrives, a buck has a fire in his belly and he's ready to go. Starting a few days before and ending about 10 days after the rutting moon, the woods will be humming. Whether you call the activity bonkers, ballistic or frenzied, this is when hunters dream of being in the woods. If you have a two-week period for vacation, this is when to take it. Write it down or etch it in stone, because you don't want to miss this handful of days.

By the time the post-rut moon inches over the horizon, the rutting game is about over. Any bucks left standing are worn out. And if these survivors live in "run-and-gun" and "brown-it's-down" country where gun-hunting pressure is intense, they will be so secretive that you'll need radar to find them.

In Chapter 16, I'll discuss when the seeking/chasing, scraping and breeding phases of the rut will occur through 2020, as well as when these phases occurred in the years since 1995 when Laroche and I began writing about the moon's effect on whitetails.

The past will give you some history so you'll have background for the future.

CHAPTER 8

Hunting Strategies for the Pre-Rut Moon

Historically, the whitetail's pre-rut has generated limited interest among deer hunters. Many view it as nothing more than a warm-up stage, a time to see what's in the woods, and to start thinking about big bucks and November's opportunities.

Though many bow seasons in North America open in late August and early September, this chapter will deal with the pre-rut period, which is the first full moon after the fall equinox in late September. This period begins a couple of days before the pre-rut moon and ends about seven days before the rutting moon.

During this time, a buck's behavior is laid back, as described in Chapter 6. As September eases into October, the whitetail's thick winter coat grows in. This heavier coat, coupled with autumn's warm days, causes whitetails to be less active in daylight hours. As a result, they move at the edge of day and feed at night. Except for the latter stages of this period, bucks seldom leave their core area, which is often little more than one square mile. On the other hand, does seem to continue their normal movements. With doe sightings normal and buck sightings rare, hunting can be frustrating.

Various studies have repeatedly shown that bucks travel little until mid-October when the rpm increase on their rutting engines. Seven years ago, the New York State Department of Environmental Conservation began radio-collaring whitetails near my home in western New York to determine their movement patterns. Our farm is within the study area, and it's fascinating to see how these deer move throughout the year. The study parallels findings of previous research in that bucks travel little during the summer, and stay in a small area until mid-October.

I've traveled often with the biologists to monitor the bucks, and it's amazing how predictable they are in late summer and early fall. They're in the same vicinity day after day, living where adequate cover, food and water are nearby. Though the bucks are secretive at this time, an added bonus of hunting the pre-rut is that bucks are often in bachelor groups.

As with humans, whitetails have a sweet tooth. Hunting in and around apple orchards can offer great opportunities at this time of the year.

During September and October, white-tailed deer gravitate to nutritional food sources like clover and alfalfa.

It's not uncommon to find several bucks together when the pre-rut moon arrives. I've had up to seven bucks walk past my stand at this time.

Within a week after the pre-rut moon, the bachelor groups have disintegrated. A big reason for that, I believe, is that about 10 percent of the does cue off the pre-rut moon, come into estrous, and are bred a week or two afterward. Some hunters call this the "false rut" because it appears that things will explode. However, because few does cycle at this time, it only amounts to a flare-up.

Follow the Food Chain

The pre-rut moon period, for the most part, is a leisure time for whitetails. For this reason, I hunt food sources heavily at this time. Research shows it's not uncommon for bucks to increase their body weight by 25 percent during August, September and October. The increased food intake occurs because once the rutting moon arrives and the rut becomes full blown, bucks do little eating as the breeding urge overwhelms them. As a result, they're determined and predictable in their quest for food during September and October. With this in mind, I begin scouting for food sources in late July and early August. Where I live in the Northeast, I try to find sites with an abundance of acorns, beechnuts, apples, corn,

This bow-hunter is about to shoot at a buck that was gorging in an apple orchard. For the best deer activity, I always look for apple orchards that are old and abandoned.

Acorns provide an excellent source of carbohydrates for deer. Whether they come from a red or white oak, acorns will always draw a deer's attention and be among its favorite foods.

clover, alfalfa and other foods.

Because of the whitetail's innate ability to determine which food is the most nutritious, I spend a lot of time scouting for the best foods. Throughout summer, I scout clover and alfalfa fields. Each of these foods has a protein value of about 20 percent, and whitetails gravitate to them. Most of my hayfield scouting consists of glassing long-distance at dusk with binoculars. By keeping my distance from the wood's edge, I can scout without pressuring the bucks. The cover around a hayfield is a key in determining if a hayfield is a candidate for early-season bow-hunting.

Aerial photos reveal a great deal about a wooded area's natural funnels or inside corners, where bucks often enter the field. I'll occasionally check the field's edge for droppings to determine how many deer are using the site. However, I try to limit my close-quarter scouting so I don't pressure bucks I want to hunt later.

I also spend August's warm days checking the area's corn crop. During late summer, deer activity will not be high around cornfields, except for fields with early-maturing sweet corn. Once October arrives,

In areas with heavy mast crops, the best time to hunt during the pre-rut moon period will be two hours on both sides of daylight. This is a time when the air is still cool or cooling off, making it more comfortable for whitetails to move.

and field-corn starts maturing, deer sightings increase dramatically. As with hayfields, I look for cornfields that have attractive cover and natural funnels around them. Cornfields with adequate cover can become real buck magnets throughout fall, providing secure cover is nearby.

Of all the food sources available to whitetails, none is as attractive as acorns. Acorns are nutritious, and regardless of whether they're white or red, deer abandon other foods in favor of acorns because they're high in fat-building carbohydrates. The fat that deer put on helps get them through winter. Always remember, though, that acorns can be cyclical. Just because the oaks bore acorns last year doesn't mean they'll bear a heavy crop this year.

I begin scouting for acorns in earnest about Aug. 1 by glassing the oak canopy with binoculars. That helps me determine what kind of acorn crop to expect. Also, if you find oak stands in a natural funnel, the potential for deer sightings increases dramatically. In my area, acorns begin falling in late August, and bucks quickly take advantage of the new food supply. By checking for droppings, you can get an idea how many deer are using the location and plan your hunts accordingly.

Whitetails will begin feeding heavily in cornfields once the corn begins maturing. Hunting along deer trails that lead to such fields can offer great hunting opportunities.

Always remember that whitetails have a sweet tooth. That's probably why more pre-rut moon bucks have been killed in or near apple orchards than any other place. During early autumn, deer habitat is changing, and most plants are stalky (very high in fiber) and not to a deer's liking. Consequently, when apples begin falling, whitetails find them in a hurry. I pay especially close attention to old, abandoned apple orchards choked with thick brush.

The Ambush

When scouting during the pre-rut moon period, I look for well-worn trails near food sources. I also try to determine how far deer are traveling from their bedding areas without actually going into them. The best time to scout is during late morning or midday when bucks are bedded. If deer have to travel far to get from the bedding area to their food source, you'll see few deer in daylight. The key is to place your stand as close to the bedding area as possible without actually being in the bedroom. This can be tricky. If you pressure bucks too much, especially mature bucks, they'll become nocturnal. There is no harder buck to hunt than one that

A whitetail can detect odors at least 100 times better than humans. To beat a mature buck, you must beat his nose. Always hunt with the wind in your favor when choosing a stand. If the wind doesn't favor a site, hunt somewhere else.

When I place my stands, I look for trees where stands can be placed at least 15 feet high and no more than 15 yards off the downwind side of the trail. And I want a tree that is large enough to break up my outline.

moves mostly at night. By setting up close to the bedding area, you can intercept bucks as they head for food sources at the end of the day.

If I'm hunting an apple orchard, I scout for well-worn trails near the heaviest fruit-bearing trees. Also, I begin looking for a good tree-stand site when the apples start falling because bucks will be there to gorge. If it appears bucks are bedding close to the orchard, I try to hang a portable stand in the orchard if a given tree offers potential. However, if several trees are bearing apples, my strategy changes. I then place my stand where deer must pass to reach the orchard. Several trails usually lead into an orchard, so you need to scout thoroughly to locate the ones that get the most use.

When I place my stands, I look for trees where stands can be placed at least 15 feet high, and no more than 15 yards off the downwind side of the trail. And I want a tree that will break up my outline. Nothing is worse than looking like a lollipop in the sky. If a tree doesn't offer natural concealment, I hang evergreen boughs behind me to break up my outline.

I prefer intercepting bucks before they get to the apple trees because, once they get into an orchard, it's nearly impossible to determine which way they'll go. A whitetail will usually gravitate to whatever tree drops the most apples on a given day.

If the bedding area around a food source is not well defined, deer will come to feed from any direction. If this happens, I'll work the wind and hang the stand where I find the most sign, and move accordingly if needed. The sign I'm looking for is heavy mast on the ground and concentrations of droppings. These two things will give me an idea of how the area is being used.

When choosing early-season stand sites, focus on areas where food, water and cover are all nearby. Remember, in most areas a white-tailed buck travels little from early September until late October, so if your stand is in an area where a buck can easily meet his three necessities, your opportunities will increase.

Hanging tree stands along well-used trails leading to the field can provide a good deal of action when hunting near hayfields, cornfields, or

Trail-hunting is most productive during the pre-rut. It often pays to set up as close to the deer's bedding area as possible without spooking them. If they move late in the day, you might catch them before it gets too dark to shoot.

> *If I see a buck walking through the woods, I use a grunt to stop him. If he's interested, one to three grunts should get him stopped and coming my way. If a buck responds, I stop calling when he starts heading in my direction.*

grain fields. Also, trails that meander toward bedding areas offer excellent opportunities for stands, especially where several trails merge.

Teasing Tactics

Though rattling and calling with a grunt tube are generally considered rut strategies, I use both during the pre-rut moon period. Because bucks spar often during early fall, my rattling tactics revolve around imitating two bucks sparring. I gently tickle my rattling antlers together in a non-aggressive manner at a medium volume. My sparring sequences last less than five minutes. I repeat the process an hour later if I receive no response. I usually limit this type of rattling to the first and last two hours of the day.

My calling strategy during this period is confined to trailing grunts (short, medium tone grunts with about a second or two between them) and the doe bleat, which is a good locator call. If I see a buck walking through the woods, I'll often use a trail grunt to get him stopped. If he's interested, one to three grunts should get him stopped and coming my way. If a buck responds, it's important to stop calling when he starts heading in your direction. If you don't, you'll risk having him spot you.

I'll use the doe bleat if the action is slow and I'm trying to lure an unseen buck that might be just out of sight. Generally, I'll give two or three bleats, and repeat the process every 30 to 45 minutes if nothing responds.

Beating a Buck's Nose

Again, always make sure your stand is downwind of where you expect to hunt. If it isn't, move it. Nothing will destroy preseason scouting faster than not working the wind in your favor. There are many ways to fool a whitetail, but his nose is not one of them. Generally, there is more moisture in the air in the morning than the afternoon. As a result, scent lingers longer in the morning. Also, I prefer a little breeze as opposed to none at all. Why? A light, steady breeze will carry scent directly downwind and away from where you expect a buck to show up. If there is no wind, your scent will ride the thermals (drafts caused by the heating and

The key to hunting the pre-rut moon period is to hunt with food sources in mind. I start scouting for acorns in early August. I glass the oaks' treetops to gauge how much mast they'll produce. Acorns in my region usually start dropping in late August.

cooling of the earth's surface) around your stand and cause problems.

Hunting in hilly country can be challenging, because terrain causes winds to constantly change direction. However, on days with no wind, hilly country can be hunted effectively if you remember a couple of things about thermals. In the morning as the ground warms, air will rise, causing the thermals to blow uphill. In the afternoon and evening as the ground cools, the wind reverses and blows downhill.

Over the past few years, scent-killers have become popular. By spraying a good scent eliminator on clothing and wiping a cloth sprayed with scent-eliminator over your neck and face, much human odor can be eliminated. I also wear a Scent-Lok type suit to ensure my scent is contained as much as possible.

However, if you don't control your breath odor, it doesn't matter what kind of scent precautions you take. Breath odors spook deer as quickly as body and equipment odors. A person exhales 250 liters of air into the environment around them every hour, which will turn a deer inside out when it smells it.

Breath odors spook deer as quickly as body and equipment odors. A person exhales 250 liters of air into the environment around him every hour, which will turn a deer inside out when it smells it.

Breath odor can be neutralized two ways. First, chlorophyll tablets can be purchased in most drug stores, and do a good job of neutralizing breath odors. Perhaps an easier way to eliminate foul breath — providing you have apple trees where you hunt — is to carry an apple with you and suck on a chunk of it as you sit on your stand. Apples are "nature's tooth brush," and will take away unwanted breath odors.

When to Hunt

Unlike the rutting-moon period when bucks are going ballistic and are constantly on the move, deer activity during the pre-rut moon days can be slow to nonexistent. During this time, I've found evening sits more productive than morning watches. I've also found that when the pre-rut moon shines full, evening activity can be excellent, especially when the pre-rut moon is creeping over the eastern horizon and the sun is falling in the western sky at the same time. When that occurs, an evening hunt can be memorable.

Late-day movement at this time has much to do with the fact deer have been bedded all day in the warm temperatures, and are eager to start feeding as the coolness of night approaches.

And lastly, remember that when the pre-rut moon occurs, the stage is set for rapid changes in the deer woods as a buck's desires change from food to sex. Chance favors the prepared hunter. Being ready for the change and preparing for what the rutting moon will bring will put you in position to kill the buck of your dreams.

CHAPTER 9

Hunting Strategies for the Rutting Moon

Although white-tailed bucks scrape, rub and chase does, it's the does that create the rut. Therefore, my hunting strategy revolves around pursuing mature white-tailed bucks as they react and interact with doe groups.

As already mentioned, a whitetail's rutting switch is thrown from mid- to late October (in the North). For the next 30 days, a buck develops an ever-increasing case of "sexitis." During this time, bucks let their guard down and become vulnerable. Once the rut's breeding phase is full blown, a buck becomes harder to hunt because he's around does. So, the best window of opportunity for hunting the rutting moon, which is the second full moon after the fall equinox, is about three days before the full moon until about seven to 10 days afterward.

A whitetail's range can be broken into three zones: feeding, bedding and the area in between, which I call the transition zone. If pressure isn't severe, the transition zone is where I ambush the most bucks during the rut. Why? For five reasons:

○ Mature bucks seldom frequent feeding areas during daylight hours.

○ If they do, does are usually nearby and the scene can resemble a fire drill when chasing starts.

○ With several deer in the feeding area, you have all kinds of eyes to contend with before the moment of truth arrives.

○ You must stay out of the bedding area to keep a slammer buck from changing its habits.

○ The transition zone is where most rutting sign will be found and where a buck is most vulnerable.

Most of the time I hunt transition zones during the rutting moon period to kill a mature buck. Generally, a transition zone is anywhere from 50 yards to over a mile in length. It all depends on how far the bedding area is from the feeding area, or how far one bedding area is from another. If a transition zone is thick or happens to be a natural funnel, your chances for success increase.

When the rutting moon is full, the stage is set for bucks to go bonkers.

If conditions and habitat are right, a number of trails will pass through a transition zone. It's along and near these trails that I look for key rutting sign in mid-October. As with pre-rut scouting, I go into these areas between mid-morning and noon as inconspicuously as possible while searching for sign. Generally, I don't have to spend a lot of time in any one location because my off-season scouting has shown me where to look.

Scrapes: The Whitetail's Billboard

As the rutting moon arrives and the rut intensifies, three types of scrapes show up: boundary, secondary and primary. Boundary scrapes are made randomly as bucks travel through their territory. These scrapes often show up along the edges of fields, fence rows, old roadways and along creeks. Yearling bucks make many (but not all) boundary scrapes as they try to figure out their first rut. Therefore, I pay little attention to these scrapes except for checking the track sizes. If the track is more than 2¼ inches wide (with no more than a ¼-inch split in the toes) the buck probably is mature and weighs more than 175 pounds.

Secondary scrapes are generally found along well-used trails between bedding and feeding areas, and they can offer an excellent chance to kill

If a whitetail track is more than 2¼ inches wide with more than ¼-inch split between the toes, it's an indication the deer weighs more than 175 pounds. Less than 10 percent of all white-tailed does weigh more than 160 pounds, so a track exceeding these dimensions indicates a mature buck.

bucks. In many instances, bucks make a line of these scrapes (20 to 50 yards apart) between the bedding and feeding areas. Because these scrapes are on trails, bucks frequently rework and freshen them. I've probably killed more bucks along secondary scrapes than at any other place.

The "mother lode" of scrapes is the primary scrape. Unfortunately, these scrapes are often few and far between because it takes a mature buck population for them to exist. The primary scrape is the true "bus station" for white-tailed bucks, and it is something all hunters yearn to find. Primary scrapes are normally found in strategic locations during the rut. You'll find well-worn trails to primary scrapes, and more often than not, these scrapes will be in thick cover where mature bucks feel secure.

Become a Scrape Doctor

I try to plan my scrape hunting around three or four good scrape locations, rotating between them so as not to over-hunt any one. Because I'll be rattling and calling from these ambush points, I look for hot scrapes

Doctoring scrapes is an excellent way to enhance a scrape's attractiveness.

When applying scent to a canister, make sure no human odor is left behind.

with medium to heavy cover. If I find a highly used area that looks good for an ambush, I'll make a licking branch where I'd like a buck to stop. I do this by cutting a fresh branch from a tree and securing it about five feet off the ground. This works great along a trail where you know a buck must stop for you to get a clean, standing shot. If bucks like the licking branch, which is usually the case, a scrape will open under it.

Once I make a decision on a scrape location, I begin doctoring it. Not all scrapes are candidates for doctoring or for using lures around them. I've found that huntable scrapes need to be on flat or fairly flat ground in well-used travel corridors (funnels) that give bucks a sense of security.

To make lures shine, find a primary or secondary scrape to hunt over. The most critical aspect of scrape hunting is to make sure there is a good licking branch above the scrape. Remember, whitetails work the licking branch far more than they paw the ground.

Using lures to attract bucks was in part an outgrowth of my days as a fox trapper. Through experiences as a trapper, I realized my chances of trapping a fox increased according to the amount of fox scent I had around the set. Because of this, I felt confident that deer could be lured into bow, gun and camera range in much the same way. By using the premise that a

Scent pads like this are great ways to bring a buck close to your stand.

whitetail scrape resembled a fox set, I've been successful at making certain scraping locations into whitetail magnets by using lures and attractive licking branches.

When I trapped fox I used to make the set hotter by applying liberal amounts of red fox urine around the bait and set. Also, if I caught a fox I'd try not to disturb the set because I knew the fox's odor would enhance the set, making it more attractive to other foxes in the area. I'd also make a scent post near the set so a roving fox could smell the locations from a distance. In all cases, I made sure I left no human odor behind.

I share this fox trapping

Stand location is critical during the rut. I hang my stands downwind, 15 to 20 feet high, and within my shooting limits of where I expect to see the buck.

scenario because I use the same principle when using deer lures around scrapes and when making scent trails. I begin by making sure I leave no human odor around the scrape I intend to doctor. I use 35 mm film canisters with the tops half perforated, and I then boil the canisters in water to kill human odors. I place three cotton balls inside each canister to prepare them for hanging above the licking branch.

I also wear rubber boots when hunting around doctored scrapes and when going to and from the area I intend to hunt. To eliminate human scent on my boots, I periodically wash them with soap and warm water, then rinse them with boiling hot water. I also use latex gloves when tying scent canisters above the scrape.

Concocting Lures

Since the late 1980s, I've used two lures to hunt whitetails. I make one from pure whitetail urine and vaginal discharge from Holstein cows.

My favorite place to ambush a rutting buck is in the transition zone, which is between the bedding and feeding areas.

Using the vaginal discharge of dairy cows probably comes as a shock to some. I began using it in 1982 (I gave it the name *white lightning*) when I heard of a dairy farmer from a neighboring state who had bow-killed some impressive whitetails while using it. He had collected and used only the discharge from cows in the peak of their estrous cycle. If I cannot get fresh whitetail urine to mix with the discharge, I use fresh Holstein urine.

A key aspect of using lures successfully is to keep them fresh. Regardless of what lure is used, freshness is essential because pheromones in the lure dissipate rapidly. Because of this, I refrigerate my lures and try to use them within a week to 10 days. I never carry them over to the next year.

To doctor the scrape, I tie one or two scent-laden canisters on the licking branch, at least six feet off the ground. Then, I fill the canister with lure. I do this with an eyedropper, inserting the lure through the large hole in the side of the canister. This can be expensive because it takes about one ounce of lure to fill the film canister.

Many will wonder why I use vaginal discharge lure above the scrape. After all, does and bucks urinate on the ground, not in the tree branches,

When a buck makes a rub, he's not only leaving his visual "calling card," but also scent from his forehead, nasal and preorbital gland.

If you ever find a rub line like this, begin hunting it ASAP. It's a big buck's travel corridor.

right? Well, I used to think this way but after a good deal of experimenting I've found that bucks aren't concerned about where the smell is coming from. Having the canister in the air allows bucks to smell the lure from farther away.

Lastly, I do one rather radical thing at the scrape site during the doctoring process. When I'm hunting over a particular scrape I'll urinate onto it after my morning sit. The tactic might be a surprise to some, but I've used it for nearly 15 years, and like many hunters, I've found it works well. However, if you are on medication, don't use your own urine because medication can foul the urine and spook nearby deer.

Using Human Urine

Fox trapping taught me that I was more successful when I made a set as powerful smelling as possible. By urinating into a scrape, I'm able to put more than 10 ounces of "lure" onto the fresh earth. If I were to place commercial lure on the scrape, it would cost roughly $75 ($7 per ounce) every time I doctored it. However, this isn't the only reason I do it. I do it because it works.

Nearly 65 percent to 70 percent of scraping is done under the cover of darkness.

Both human and whitetail urine are animal urine by nature. Each gives off the same ammonia smell after being exposed to dirt and air for a while. I've doctored scrapes in this fashion all across North America, and never once have I seen a buck become alarmed. In all cases, bucks smelled the ground and worked the scrape before moving on. Using your own urine is a way to make a scrape hotter without killing your pocketbook.

I never use human urine to doctor scrapes at the end of the day. Whitetails are on the prowl at dusk, and I don't want to risk spooking them before the urine breaks down. Also, I never use human urine in scent canisters that are for vaginal discharge lures.

To keep the scrapes as hot as possible I replenish the lure in the canisters every other day. The important thing is to keep the odor strong. Also, fresh earth under the scrape seems to be an attractant, so I make sure that the scrape beneath the licking branch is kept roughed up and free of debris.

Build a Better Mouse Trap with a Scent Trail

I also use lures to make scent trails in and out of the woods I'm hunting. This tactic is used by deer hunters across America, and there are a number of ways to lay a good scent trail. Some hunters drag a scent-laden rag behind them as they walk into the woods, while others use scent pads on the bottoms of their boots. I periodically squirt estrous lure on the bottoms of my rubber boots as I walk into my stand, starting the process when I'm within 100 to 150 yards of where I intend to hunt. I walk past the stand to make the trail where I would like a buck to follow, then backtrack and get into the stand.

The Stand Location

Setting up the ambush over a hot scrape or scrape line can be tricky. First, try to find a hot scrape as close to a bedding area as possible, or in a funnel that has a lot of use. By doing so, you'll be in better position to intercept a buck visiting his scrape during daylight hours. Remember, nearly 65 percent to 70 percent of scraping is done under the cover of

Never climb into a stand during the rut without a deer call. Next to your weapon, it's the most important piece of equipment you have.

During the chase phase of the rut, I've had this happen many times. The bow-hunter is grunting and the buck is looking for the source of the sound.

darkness, so by being close to the bedding area, you can intercept a mature buck when he leaves his bedroom at the end of the day. If you set up too far from a bedding area, the buck won't reach you before quitting time. The same holds true in the morning, though it is not as critical because during the chase phase of the rut, bucks are on the prowl until midday. By being close to the bedding area, you will catch a buck returning to his bedroom.

Stand placement in relation to the scrape is critical when bow-hunting. Terrain often dictates where this will be. I set up 20 to 30 yards downwind from the scrape rather than right on top of it. Of course, gun hunting over scrapes is a whole different ball game that doesn't require detailed preparation because distance isn't a factor.

As I mentioned before, I like to hang a stand in fairly thick cover so I can incorporate calling techniques with the scraping process. When rattling, you need to obstruct a buck's view when he looks for the two combatants. Because I'm usually set up in thick cover, I don't go past 15 to 18 feet high with my stands. Any higher, and tree branches and other foliage will be in your way. Also, few people feel comfortable in a stand

Antler rattling can be exciting and challenging during the 10-day period just before full-blown breeding begins.

that's 20 feet high or more. When bow-hunting in close quarters near scrapes, I seldom sit when on stand because I've learned deer can surprise you at any time. Standing also gives me more shooting angles. The moment of truth can be a bang-bang affair, and by standing, you're better prepared for the magic moment.

Importance of Hunting Rubs and Rub Lines

Often, where you find scraping you'll find rubbing. They go hand in hand, so when you find heavy rubbing in an area of heavy scraping your chances of success increase greatly. I always look for traditional signpost rubs wherever I hunt. Unfortunately it takes a good population of mature bucks for a true traditional signpost rub to exist, so, in most of the whitetail's range, where 80 percent of the buck kill is yearlings, there are no signpost rubs. But if you find one, it's a real hotspot and a prime hunting location.

If a signpost rub cannot be found, look for big rubs, rub lines and clusters of rubs in the transition zone. Rub lines often reveal the way a buck was traveling. If the scarred side of the tree faces the feeding area, the rub

Rattling from a tree stand provides the best opportunity because a buck will have a difficult time spotting you.

Because fighting can be intense during the chase phase of the rut, rattling can work well.

was probably made in the morning when the buck returned to his bedding area. If the scar faces the bedding area, the rubs were undoubtedly made when the buck exited in the evening.

If there is a definite line of big rubs in an area, a stand should be hung downwind of it. Such a rub line is a visual aid showing the area where a buck likes to travel.

One piece of rubbing sign that gets my attention in a scraping area is a cluster of rubs. When you find a cluster of rubs in a prime scraping area or an active funnel, you know there are a lot of bucks around. And if there is a good population of does, there's even more reason to be excited. Heavy rubbing by bucks leaves pheromones that induce does to come into estrus. With doe groups in the area, the chance of killing a buck increases dramatically as the rut moves through the chase phase and then climaxes with the breeding phase.

Calling All Bucks

Whitetails are no different from other animals in that they are curious creatures. Throughout their lives they communicate with each other using

Regardless of where I hunt in North America, I find that for every buck I rattle in, 10 to 15 will come to grunting and bleating.

a variety of bleats, grunts and snorts. For the first six months of life, fawns bleat and mew to their mothers. Adult bucks and does also communicate with each other by grunting and bleating. And, of course, whitetails use the snort to alert other deer of danger. During the rutting moon, when the rut is blooming, bucks also respond to the sound of two bucks fighting. Using antlers, grunt tubes and other calls to communicate with whitetails at this time can be challenging, exciting, and on occasion, very productive.

Calling

When I began calling deer, I only used antlers. Though there were successes, it wasn't until I began using a grunt tube, alone and in conjunction with antlers, that my success at luring deer close increased significantly. During the last 14 years, I've discovered that deer are more responsive to a call than anything else. For this reason my grunt tube goes with me whether I'm hunting with gun, bow or camera. Regardless of where I hunt in North America, I find that for every buck I rattle in, 10 to 15 will come to grunting and bleating.

Whether you are a novice or seasoned veteran, it's important to realize that you don't need to know how to make every vocalization of a whitetail. As a seminar speaker, I urge hunters to keep calling simple. Commercial deer calls that are capable of making a whole range of calls have not been around very long. Though researchers isolated about 400 different sounds of a whitetail when a vocalization study was done in 1984, it isn't necessary for you to know every one. The key is to be able to master two or three and know how and when to use them.

My favorite calls are the bleat, trailing grunt and tending grunt. I find the bleat to be a good locator call, much like a turkey yelp. I often use the bleat a couple of times just before and after I do a rattling sequence. I'll also use it when the action is slow and I haven't seen deer in a while. Basically it sounds like *neeeaah*.

The trailing grunt is a short grunt that bucks make when traveling through the woods or when around other deer. It's not uncommon for a rut-crazed buck to make a short grunt every one to 10 steps if he's in the

The aftermath of a vicious buck fight can be incredible. I took this photo moments after the conclusion of a fight. For more than 20 minutes, this buck stood motionless, trying to get its strength back.

right mood. If I see a buck walking through the woods, I'll use this grunt to stop him and to coax him in my direction. This is also a call that I use when no deer are in sight. If a buck is sexually active but not with a doe, there is a good chance he'll respond to a grunt.

The tending grunt can be a lethal weapon if used properly. When a buck is with a hot doe and is either frustrated by her rejections or is interrupted by another buck, he'll make a grunt that has a ticking cadence. If I'm hunting in thick cover and a buck walks through, I'll use a tending grunt to bring him to my stand. This is a great call to use when bucks are on the move and the rut is boiling over.

Rattling

During the rutting moon, bucks are very aggressive. Often, all it takes for a fight to occur is for one buck to look at another buck the wrong way. Over the years I've found that the best time to use antlers to bring a buck close to my stand is from about a week before the rutting moon until the third phase of the moon, which is seven days after the full moon. The

When breeding begins, hunting gets tough, unless you have a hot doe near your tree stand.

seven days that follow the rutting moon are the best time during the period.

When I rattle, I do it aggressively with a sequence that seldom lasts longer than five minutes. Few fights I've witnessed have ever lasted longer, so I keep it short and loud and make it as aggressive sounding as possible. Generally, I rattle for a minute and half, pause for 30 seconds, rattle for a minute and a half, pause for 30 seconds then end the sequence by rattling for a minute and a half. I also found that rattling two hours before or after daylight works best. But don't rule out midday, because I've rattled in some nice bucks when the rutting moon is full.

When rattling, do it in the thickest cover possible, especially if you're bow-hunting. When a buck responds to antlers he will come in cautious, looking for the combatants. If he can't see them, he'll usually hang up. Thick cover forces him to come closer. Though you can't make as many natural sounds, like breaking branches and raking the ground, rattling from a tree stand gives greater concealment, allows you to see the buck coming, and keeps the incoming buck from spotting you.

Deercoying can add an exciting dimension to the hunt.

I realized that to be more successful, I'd have to make approaching bucks more curious and less cautious about the decoy I was using for bow-hunting.

Tease with a "Deke"

A great way to attract wary bucks during the rutting moon is with decoys. I began extensively using decoys shortly after Flambeau developed its 3-D doe decoy in 1989. Since then, I've hunted and photographed over decoys from New York to Texas to Saskatchewan. In the beginning I thought, "This is too easy." I quickly learned that there were many do's and don'ts in using decoys. I've found the rutting moon period, when bucks go bonkers, to be the best time for decoys, be it buck or doe.

Because incoming whitetail bucks almost always circle the decoy, I prefer 3-D units over silhouettes. As good as today's decoys appear to be, their most common shortcoming is a lack of motion. Without some kind of motion, decoys, at best, work only about 50 percent of the time. From early on, I realized that to be more successful I'd have to make approaching bucks more curious and less cautious about the decoy I was using for bow-hunting.

Though it took a little effort, I remedied the situation by attaching a paper clamp to the rump of the decoy. I use the clamp to hold a white handkerchief, and I tie monofilament fishing line to the handkerchief and run the line to my tree stand. Then, after attaching the line to my boot I'm able to add just enough tail flickering to the decoy for a buck to think the decoy is real.

Deer do not pick up a decoy's presence easily if the decoy is in thick brush. So for best results, decoys should be placed at the edge of a field or in a well traveled funnel where deer can easily see them.

Because 3-D decoys can be cumbersome and noisy to assemble, think through how you're going to get them to your hunting position. If you must assemble them every time you use them, do the assembly at least 100 yards from where you intend to hunt. Nothing will ruin a set-up quicker than plastic parts banging together. Also, never leave a decoy set up when you are not hunting over it. Once a deer has been fooled by a decoy, your chances of fooling him again are almost zero.

Three things are important when readying a decoy for hunting:

○ Get rid of any human odor by spraying the decoy liberally with scent

Unless you add motion to a decoy, there is a 50/50 chance the buck will hang up and never offer a shot. Adding motion to a decoy is critical if you expect consistent success.

eliminator.

○ Make sure the decoy is anchored to the ground. The last thing you want is for it to fall over in the wind or from the soft touch of a deer.

○ Never carry a decoy without wearing blaze orange. Today's decoys are authentic looking and for this reason safety is paramount while moving them around.

Buck or doe decoy?

Whitetails will respond to buck and doe decoys. If you want to use a doe decoy, the best time is from about one week before the rutting moon until the end of the breeding period. Buck decoys work better if there is high aggression in the population, which happens when there is an abundance of mature bucks in the herd. If this is the case, a buck decoy will work well during the pre-rut and rut periods. If the area you hunt has too many does and a lot of yearling bucks, a buck decoy will not work as well as a doe decoy.

When bow-hunting with a doe decoy, avoid placing it less than 15 yards from your stand. It's far better to place the decoy 20 to 25 yards upwind of

Always remember that bucks size each other up by body, antler size or a combination of both.

your stand, with the decoy facing or quartering away from you. In most cases, a buck will circle a doe decoy, rather than coming straight to it. Also, if a buck suspects something is odd about the scene (which can often happen) it will hang up within 20 to 30 yards from the decoy. By placing the decoy about 25 yards from your stand, you will be able to get a shot when the buck hangs up. This will often be at point blank range. If a buck comes all the way to the decoy it will give you many opportunities for a broadside shot while it explores the backside of the doe decoy.

When bow-hunting with a buck decoy, I plan my strategy differently. I place the decoy about 20 yards upwind of my stand with it facing or quartering toward me. Unlike the doe decoy, where the buck approaches from the rear, a buck will usually approach a buck decoy from the front. So, it's best to have the buck decoy facing you. The antlers I use on the decoy are always representative of the area I'm hunting. In high-pressure areas where there are few mature bucks this means nothing larger than 100-class Boone-and-Crockett antlers. Always remember that bucks size each other up by body, antler size or a combination of both. This sets the tone for their aggression toward each other. Using only one antler on a buck decoy will suggest that the decoy is a fighter, thus stimulating aggression.

If you bow-hunt over a buck decoy and the approaching buck is one you want to take (and shows an aggressive "attitude") you'll have to shoot him before he reaches the decoy. If you wait for him to get to the decoy, the speed of a frenzied fight will make it impossible for a shot.

CHAPTER 10

Hunting Strategies for the Post-Rut Moon

In most parts of North America, hunting during December, when the third full moon after the fall equinox arrives, is a far cry from the slam-bang action of the previous month's rut. The differences between hunting November's rut and December's post-rut can often be as different as night and day. There are a couple of reasons for this. A whitetail's biological make-up at this time of the year and the amount of human pressure it has encountered from September to December are key factors that help explain why post-rut bucks can be the hardest of all whitetails to hunt.

As I've pointed out, Laroche and I believe that in a fine-tuned deer herd, about 70 percent to 80 percent of mature does are bred during the rutting moon period. Our findings also show that 10 percent to 15 percent of the doe population is bred during the pre-rut moon period in October. So, with 80 percent to 90 percent of the North's doe population already bred by December, the picture can look rather bleak for a hunter expecting any semblance of November's rut.

By the time a buck makes it though November's breeding ordeal and arrives at December's door, he's a far cry from the muscular rutting machine he was when the rutting moon burst onto the scene. A white-tailed buck in the post-rut has much in common with a marathon runner who's just completed a 26-mile race — he's out of gas and ready to drop. In fact, it's not uncommon to see white-tailed bucks at this time of the year on the verge of physical meltdown because of exhaustion and weight loss. So, by the time the post-rut moon hangs full in the sky, a buck's priorities have changed from sex to survival, in spite of the fact that roughly 10 percent to 15 percent of the does are yet to be bred.

Biology

There is no doubt that many hunters question a buck's decreased desire to breed in December (in the North), especially when magazines wax on the virtues of the so-called "second rut." A buck's ability to keep up the rutting chase in the post-rut moon is possible, but in most cases

As the rut winds down and the post-rut progresses, bucks move less often.

highly unlikely. Why? Research (Lambase 1972) shows that a buck's sperm count in December is about half of what it was in November. So physically, the drive isn't there. As a result, bucks are calmer, more collected animals when the post-rut moon arrives.

Because survival is now his main objective, a buck becomes a different creature in December and early January. Oh, he will still breed, and often does, but generally he isn't out looking for does the way he was in October and November. Rather, he feeds, rests and takes what comes his way.

When December arrives in the North, the entire deer family group gravitates toward known food sources, such as cornfields in farm country or cedar swamp yarding areas in wilderness regions. The main objective of bucks and does during this time is food, food, food. As a result, trying to hunt rub and scrape lines as you did in October and November is, for the most part, a waste of time.

Man's Influence on the Post-Rut

In addition to being worn out and hungry, the whitetail has another thing that keeps him from moving about: the constant presence of man.

During the post-rut period about 10 percent of does are bred. However, breeding behavior will be only a fraction of what it was during the rut.

During the post-rut period, scraping behavior will be sporadic.

You can find breeding action by hunting doe groups during the post-rut period.

During September, October and November, hunter pressure forces surviving bucks to become nocturnal. When formulating a hunting strategy for nocturnal post-rut bucks, it's important to understand that all white-tailed bucks are not the same. They fall into two categories, yearlings and adults. This is especially evident in areas where hunting pressure is heavy.

Yearling bucks are much easier to hunt, and it takes a lot of pressure for them to become truly nocturnal. The sex urge in first breeding season overwhelms most yearling's, keeping them constantly on the move. This makes yearlings huntable even in the post-rut. However, if a buck is lucky enough to survive his yearling season, he becomes a totally different animal the second season when he is 2½ years old. These deer, as well as older bucks, really go underground in the post-rut.

Contrary to popular belief among hunters, bucks do not move out of the country when hunting pressure increases. Telemetry studies conducted throughout North America indicate that whitetails do not abandon their core range during hunting season. Bucks simply hunker down, find the thickest cover possible, and limit their movements to nighttime or the fringes of daylight. Couple this with a buck's weakened,

The best hunting opportunities in the post-rut period will be near food sources.

rut-ravaged body, and it's easy to see why hunting the post-rut is the most challenging time to bag a buck.

Hunting Strategy

I am an opportunist when it comes to hunting right after November's rut. Though does will be bred during this time, I know behavior will be much different. I intensely hunt food sources close to thick cover. This is the heart and soul of hunting the late season, or post-rut. By concentrating on food sources and bedding areas, I'm able to get close to doe groups and bucks that have survived to this point in the season. Remember, does, and particularly bucks, need to gain and maintain body weight to survive winter, so everything else takes a back seat to food — even sex.

To be successful, hunting post-rut nocturnal bucks requires that you scout smart for them. For years, I hunted the same way the entire deer season. This amounted to hunting the scrape areas I'd found early in the season. The only thing wrong was that once full-blown breeding arrived and gun season began, scraping activity dwindled to almost nothing. And as gun season progressed, deer sightings decreased significantly.

Then I changed my way of thinking. My buck sightings and opportunities increased dramatically when I began wondering, "If I were a buck, where would I be hiding when the tail end of the season arrived?" As might be expected, I looked intently at the thickest cover I could find in close proximity to known feeding areas.

Think Bed & Breakfast — Lunch & Dinner, Too!

To save time and energy, I use aerial photos and topographical maps to locate prospective bedding areas. When areas coincide with the topo map's steep elevation lines, it's an indicator of

Because hunting pressure is normally low during post-rut, tracking a buck can be a productive way to hunt and kill a trophy.

where deer will be bedded. Note that whitetails love to bed just over an edge where they can watch downwind and, at the same time, have their backs to the wind, enabling them to smell danger in the direction they can't see.

A bedding area's relation to food and water can't be emphasized enough, for it reveals how a buck moves to and from the bedding area. During the post-rut, try to find bedding areas that are close to the whitetail's feeding areas. Bucks are weary and don't want to travel too far for food if they can help it. As a result, you'll often find them bedding in thick cover within 200 to 300 yards of standing field crops or mast sources.

When a trail is found leading to or from a bedding area, look at the tracks closely. If most or all are heading toward the feeding area, the trail is probably being used in the evening. If the tracks indicate movement into the bedding area, the trail is being used in the morning. Knowing a

Once the rut is over and the post-rut sets in, bucks will bed for extended periods of time, rising only to stretch and eat.

whitetail's escape routes will help you   plan hunting strategies and determine ambush locations.

I plan my ambush of a post-rut buck by being as inconspicuous as possible. This means I do not spend a lot of time in the area. I hang my stand near the bedding area's known escape routes or where sign and cover is thickest. And, I hang my stands as close as I can to the known bedding area without spooking deer. In addition, I make sure the stands are hung at least a month before I intend to hunt the area. Because of their size and the amount of noise required to build them, I seldom use permanent stands when hunting nocturnal bucks in thick cover. It's just too risky. If you make too much commotion in a buck's bedroom, he'll move out. With the stand in place, I take time to cut several small shooting lanes. And lastly, I make sure I have at least two ways to get into the stand quietly. This is critical. If you rely on only one entrance and exit route, deer will figure you out in a hurry.

Though I will not dwell on this a great deal, it's important to note that a whitetail's feeding times in the post-rut can change drastically from what they were in September, October or November. In the North, where

The thing to remember is that breeding activity is very probable during the post-rut.

winter usually begins in early December, there will be more midday activity in the post-rut, especially if hunting pressure has not been intense. In my experience, the hours of 10 a.m. to 2 p.m. and 3 p.m. to nightfall have offered the greatest deer activity during the post-rut.

The Third Breeding Phase

For the most part, the primary breeding phase of the whitetail rut is over in the North by the time the post-rut moon arrives. Though November's breeding phase is but a memory, there is still a wee bit of a breeding phase to come. As mentioned earlier, in a fine-tuned herd the post-rut usually sees about 10 percent to 15 percent of the does bred. Most of this is a result of a biological phenomena brought on by a healthy deer herd.

If fawn births are on schedule, meaning mid-May to early June, and favorable conditions are present in the form of good nutrition, many doe fawns will come into estrus in December. Our research shows that some of these fawns and yearling does are cuing off the post-rut moon and being bred seven to 14 days thereafter.

I know that when the post-rut moon, the third full moon after the fall equinox, is full, there should be some breeding activity that follows. However, don't expect this to be nearly as spectacular as what took place in November. Unfortunately, by the time the post-rut rolls around, the adult buck population has thinned significantly. As a result, the post-rut breeding phase might not be noticeable, unless more than one buck is vying for the same doe. Then a little chasing could take place.

The thing to remember is that breeding activity is very probable during the post-rut. Concentrate on doe groups because if one doe happens to come into estrus and there are bucks in the area, you'll be in position to take advantage of it. Actually, I don't plan my hunts around this. Instead I concentrate on hunting food and bedding sources where there are concentrations of deer.

Weather can be unpredictable in the North toward the end of hunting season. Conditions like this almost mandate still-hunting.

During the post-rut, bucks revert to pre-rut behaviors. These two bucks have re-formed their bachelor group and are sparring.

Tease Them Into Range

The use of antlers and deer calls is associated with hunting the rut. There's no question that November is the time when both work best. However, don't put them away, because the post-rut is also a great time to use antlers and calls. Over the years, I've had many close encounters with bucks because I rattled and called.

When I do rattle during the post-rut, I make more of a sparring noise than the noises I would make when simulating a full-blown fight. Two bucks will seldom really go at it after the flurry of the rut is past, so I find less noise to be better. I might lightly tickle the tines or bang the antlers slowly together. Typically, I do this for about five to 10 minutes, and in some cases not more than a minute or two.

The latter might take place if I can actually see a buck from my stand location. If this happens, I want him to know something is going on in my direction. If he heads for me, I stop the simulated sparring and get ready.

Also, set-up is critical when rattling in the post-rut. By being close to

For the hunter with patience and the ability to withstand cold temperatures, the post-rut period offers some great rewards.

The use of antlers and deer calls is associated with hunting the rut. However, don't put them away, because the post-rut is also a great time use them.

the bedding area it isn't necessary to make the sequence loud. But it needs to be loud enough for the bedded buck, wherever he is in the bedding area, to hear it. Also, I don't like to rattle unless I'm in thick cover and have a clear shooting lane downwind from my stand, because bucks often circle downwind as they try to locate the combatants.

Though I love to use antlers in the post-rut, my call of choice is a good grunt tube. I find that grunting and bleating are successful after the rut, and I use the tube the same way I did in October and November.

Aggressive Measures

Though stand hunting is my favorite way to hunt the post-rut, silent drives in gun season can also be productive for hunting wary bucks. I'm a loner when it comes to hunting anything, and seldom do I venture into the woods with more than one person. However, late in the season when it appears all bucks have left the country, I like to put on what I call my cloverleaf tactic with another hunter. It works like this:

One hunter positions himself in a tree stand in the heart of a prime bedding area. Then, one lone still-hunter proceeds to make big loops from the stand hunter. The still-hunter hunts away from the stand, makes a big loop, then comes back. The still-hunter comes back to where he can almost see the stand, then he makes another loop, continuing the process until he has gone a full 360 degrees around the person in the stand. How far out the loop takes the still-hunter depends on the size of the bedding area, but generally the loop takes in the area about 400 yards from the stand. If you were to look at this strategy from above, it would resemble a four-leaf clover, with the stand in the middle. Over the years, I've killed several bucks using this technique. I find it to be a real ace-in-the-hole when post-rut hunting gets tough.

CHAPTER 11

What About the South?

In previous chapters I've discussed the moon research that Wayne Laroche and I have been conducting. Primarily, the project involves Northern deer, although Laroche is expanding these studies to include Southern whitetails. If you live south of the 35th latitude you'll no doubt wonder if this book applies to you after reading the first 10 chapters. The answer is yes, but there are limitations on predicting the South's rut. Why? The reasons are many, though some are more easily explained than others.

Let's start with the basics. Southern whitetails don't face the harsh winters and brutal conditions that dictate when Northern white-tailed fawns must be born to ensure survival. Severe cold and deep snows aren't part of the Southern equation, so weather isn't a factor for fawn births. Therefore, the South's rut appears to be driven by less obvious factors such as climate, genetics, nutrition, doe-to-buck ratios, and conditions caused by the sun and moon. These factors all affect when does enter estrus. In many cases, these factors work together. At times, one or two factors override all others. So, be warned — in some parts of the South, nothing makes sense when predicting the rut.

Latitude

As I discussed previously, the latitude of Northern states plays an important role in whitetail breeding dates. In contrast, Southern whitetails don't seem to require a defined window of opportunity for breeding. In fact, research shows that Southern breeding dates vary greatly. For instance, in northern and southern Alabama, the rut occurs in November, while in the central region — known as the Black Belt — the rut usually occurs after Jan. 1. In central and northern Texas, the rut occurs in mid- to late November, while in southern Texas' brush country, the rut takes place from mid- to late December. In Mississippi the rut happens about a month after it occurs in northern states.

Louisiana, meanwhile, seems to have three distinct breeding periods. In its southwestern region, peak breeding occurs from mid-September to October. In its west-central and north-central regions, breeding occurs from mid-October to November, and in its eastern region, breeding occurs from December to mid-January. How about south of the border?

Throughout the South, many hunters successfully hunt areas with heavy mast. Nutrition plays a role in the rut's timing. When nutritional values are above average, a herd's does will be healthy and will enter estrus more predictably.

In northern Mexico, the rut occurs in early January.

Because of the warm climate, the whitetail's rut can occur nearly year-round in southern Florida. The closer to the equator deer live, the less predictable the rut becomes. At the equator, whitetails breed year-round.

Genetics

At first glance, the Southern rut appears totally random. Mulling over its wide variations can cause your head to spin. Clearly, we need to look at this phenomenon more closely.

Let's consider genetics, which can significantly influence the rut's timing in Southern regions. Remember, the whitetail was nearly extinct in many regions — in both the North and South — by the late 1800s. In the decades that followed, many Southern wildlife agencies restocked whitetails with deer from outside their regions. Restocking, coupled with habitat improvements and harvest regulations, allowed herds to rebound. Georgia aggressively restocked its herd with whitetails from within its borders, as well as from Kentucky, Texas, Virginia, Wisconsin and North Carolina.

Whitetails are incredibly adaptive creatures. If they can find cover and nutritious food, they'll quickly adapt to their surroundings.

Today, Georgia's Dooly County is famous for impressive bucks. The region was once restocked with Wisconsin whitetails, which are a Northern Woodland subspecies. Could Dooly County's big bucks have resulted partly from Northern Woodland genetics? So much of the South transplanted deer with varied geographic bloodlines that it's difficult to assess genetic influences 50 to 80 years later.

Harry Jacobson, a retired professor from Mississippi State University, has long been considered one of North America's top white-tailed deer researchers. As part of his university work, Jacobson studied the rut's timing to see if it was influenced by genetics. To gain such insights, Jacobson paired Michigan whitetails, which are November breeders, with Mississippi deer, which are December-January breeders. Jacobson believed that if there was a genetic link in breeding dates, it might show up in the offspring in the form of intermediate breeding dates. This was indeed the case, which helped shed light on why the rut's timing varies so greatly across the South.

Nutrition

Genetics aren't the only factor in the Southern equation. Whitetails are incredibly adaptive creatures. If they can find cover and nutritious food, they'll quickly adapt to their surroundings.

Nutritional adaptation affects the rut in two ways. First, when nutrition is above average, the herd's does will be healthy, and will usually enter estrus more predictably. When food is scarce or of poor quality — whether because of drought, overpopulation or poor growing conditions — does can become malnourished, and their body rhythms can be disrupted. The rut might then be dragged out over several months.

Combine poor nutrition and overpopulation, and a host of other factors can surface. Paramount among these are problems with parasites, which make every situation worse. Disease and epidemics further stress whitetails, and in turn, throw off a doe's reproductive cycle.

Biologists have long suspected that seasonal food sources program the rut cycles of some Southern herds. Professor James Kroll believes white-

Food plot set-ups are popular throughout the South.

Scraping intensity can vary throughout the South. In some areas it peaks in November, while in others it's highest in December.

tails in southern Texas and Mexico have a December to January rut so fawns can benefit from the summer and fall hurricane season. That season brings moisture to the arid region and creates lush vegetation. Kroll points out that if fawns were born earlier, mortality would be higher. Therefore, this region's rut appears fine-tuned by climatic forces, although far different from those governing the North's rut.

Doe-to-Buck Ratios

In many parts of North America, the whitetail's sex ratio is skewed toward females. When ratios are imbalanced, breeding periods spread out, in some cases lasting 90 days. However, as the doe-to-buck ratio reaches 2-to-1 or better, interesting things happen with the rut. A Southern study that illustrates how the rut changes by altering the adult doe-to-buck ratio is taking place at South Carolina's Mount Holley Plantation. Dr. Grant Woods, a wildlife consultant with a doctorate in deer research, began his studies on the 6,000-acre plantation in 1990. At the time, Woods figured there was one adult doe for every 0.7 antlered bucks on the property. The mean breeding date in 1990 was Oct. 19. In 1996, after six years of intense management, the herd's adult doe-to-buck ratio

Like in the North, setting up over scrape lines can be a productive way to hunt wary bucks.

had changed to 1-to-1.84. This change in the adult doe-to-buck ratio moved the mean breeding date to Sept. 21, with the earliest known breeding date on Aug. 25. As a side note, Woods believes breeding dates in the North and elsewhere can be changed and sometimes made earlier if adult sex ratios are closer to 1-to-1.

Not far from Mount Holly, in Colleton County, S.C., whitetails breed one month later, even though the Colleton property has a 1-1 adult doe-to-buck ratio. Another good example of the South's rutting disparity is the Greenville area in western South Carolina. Whitetails there breed in November,

My best Southern buck was taken on the Retamosa Ranch in southern Texas.

nearly two months later than at Mount Holley, even though both sites are at roughly the same latitude.

The Ichauway Plantation in southwestern Georgia has some of the state's best deer habitat. In 1990, as the plantation began an aggressive management program, breeding occurred in late January. By 1996, the herd's adult doe-to-buck ratio was 1-to-1, and the breeding dates had moved to mid-December.

Why such disparities within these states? No one will ever know for sure. It's one of those quirks in the whitetail's world that might defy explanation. Some say it's all genetics, but while that might explain the rut in Georgia, it won't explain the differences in South Carolina, where whitetails were not restocked from other regions.

The Moon and the South

Before looking at the moon's possible influence, let's review a bit. In previous chapters, I shared my belief that the rutting moon — which is

Like scraping, rubbing intensity can vary from month to month and state to state.

In places like southern Texas, fighting can be intense during the third full moon after the autumnal equinox.

the second full moon after the fall equinox — cues most Northern does to begin entering estrus about one week after its full phase. Because I haven't collected data on does further south than about the 35th latitude, it's impossible for me to form solid opinions about the full moon's effect on a Southern doe's estrous cycle.

But in looking at information I have obtained, I'll say this: Two tenants of science are that data must be observable and testable. I've hunted whitetails in southern Texas during the brush country's rut in mid- to late December. During the five straight years I hunted several fine-tuned ranches, I recorded details meticulously. I kept journals, took hundreds of photos, conducted extensive interviews and always hunted December's full moon. This moon was the third full moon after the autumnal equinox. During those years I saw chases, fights and aggressive interaction among mature bucks. Every year the behavior was the same, but it did not fall on the same dates, probably because the full-moon phase was on different dates each year. As I reflect on my notes and check known photo dates and other clues, I now believe the southern Texas rut is guided by the full moon.

This same influence is what Laroche and I believe cues the Northern

There are many factors that affect the timing of the South's rut. In areas where restocking has taken place, genetics can alter when does enter estrus.

rut. As previously mentioned, it's Laroche's hypothesis that once short-ened daylight reaches a certain point (such as 11 1/2 hours of daylight), the stage is set for does to enter estrus. After that point, does need a cue for estrus to occur. The cue, we believe, is the full moon's light.

Strong Confidence

After working with Laroche the past several years in collecting breed-ing data, I believe his hypothesis accurately predicts rut activity for Northern whitetails. Laroche also strongly believes his hypothesis will hold true for the South. However, like all scientists, Laroche points out that there are other factors that affect the rut's breeding phase.

Among other things, I believe genetics are a factor where restocking took place. However, even when I include all these other considerations, I believe Laroche's hypothesis has merit. Once the length of daylight drops below the figure he's determined, I believe the full moon's light cues the doe population to enter estrus. The unknown key at this point is which full moon period(s) cues Southern does. From my observations, and other research from southern Texas, it appears does in this region of Texas are cued by the third full moon after the fall equinox. Only time will tell if does in other Southern states are similarly affected by the moon.

Conclusion

Does the moon accurately predict the South's rut? If you can determine which full moon is cuing does in your area, I think it does. But the South's rut won't be as easily predicted as the North's because Southern does aren't locked into conceiving fawns during a

I killed this beautiful southern Texas buck two days after the post-rut full moon.

fixed breeding window. Also, no matter how well Laroche's chart works, it's still only a prediction. Don't forget, many rut-suppressants can change the rut's timing, whether the deer live in the North or South. In the next chapter, I'll address why certain rut-suppressants play a big part in the timing of the rut.

CHAPTER 12

The Whitetail's Rut Suppressants

I'm amazed by the interest my writings about the moon have generated. When I wrote the first of several rut-related articles in 1996, I had no idea it would turn into what it has. Hunters from Maine to Iowa to South Carolina have contacted me with many questions. Most of the responses to what Laroche and I are doing have been positive. However, there are a few skeptical hunters. Usually, when a skeptic confronts me, I find out how he hunts, including everything from techniques to when he is in the field. Usually, it turns out he didn't have enough time to hunt, or he hunted where factors suppressed deer activity.

I believe the hypothesis Laroche and I have been working on is sound when all factors are equal. Unfortunately, it's difficult to find the perfect world when dealing with things like weather, temperature, human pressure, region of the country, skewed doe-to-buck ratios and food-source management, particularly where baiting is allowed. Any of these factors will suppress daytime rutting behavior, and when they are combined, things are affected even more.

This is why it's easier and more accurate to see the "all things equal" model when studying confined deer. Under controlled conditions, most suppressants are eliminated so the moon's effects on buck and doe rutting activity can be clearly observed and documented.

This doesn't mean that, because of suppressors, the moon won't affect free-ranging deer. Despite suppressants, the pre-rut, rutting and post-rut moons' effects can be documented, although they might vary. What follows are suppressants that can affect daytime activity of rutting white-tailed deer.

Weather

Anyone who's traveled to hunt white-tailed deer knows that weather and weather patterns can make or break a hunt. So, whenever I book an out-of-state whitetail hunt, I hold my breath because I know Mother Nature will likely dictate how things unfold.

Next to foul weather, nothing shuts a white-tailed buck down faster than above normal temperatures.

Unlike humans, whitetails and other wild creatures have built-in mechanisms to alert them of impending weather changes. Whitetails can detect when barometric pressure is falling, even if the sky is clear. They know when conditions are changing, and their feeding habits increase dramatically before bad weather arrives.

Through the years, I've concluded that whitetails typically move more when the barometer is moving — up or down — than when it is steady. I've noticed whitetails do not like to move when the barometer is low and steady. During this time, you'll usually find periods of high humidity with fog, haze, rain and wet snow making up the weather system. When this happens, whitetails become secretive, especially in periods of dense fog.

The sudden drop in temperature that often accompanies these fronts doesn't cause whitetails to head for thick cover. Rather, it is caused by the unsettled weather associated with the leading edge of low-pressure fronts. The greatest movement occurs if barometric pressure drops rapidly. With few exceptions, there will be little deer movement

If heavy rain or snow fall during the peak of the rut, buck activity can slow to a near halt. However, when a storm front has passed and conditions are moderate, activity will explode.

after the front arrives. Then, as the front passes and the weather returns to normal, whitetails and other wildlife start to move in search of food.

When the storm ends and the barometer begins rising, deer activity increases dramatically, providing air temperatures match the whitetail's comfort zone. Several studies have been completed regarding the effects of barometric pressure on whitetail activity. Illinois biologist Keith Thomas found that most whitetail feedings occurred when barometric pressure was between 29.80 and 30.29. When the barometer is falling or rising through this range, deer activity should be the greatest. So, be a weather watcher to ensure you have the upper hand.

Temperature

Warm temperatures shut down rutting activity in a heartbeat. Of all rut suppressors, air temperature is perhaps the most powerful influence on daytime deer activity. Other suppressors work in concert with

Any encroachment from humans — especially urbanization — will have an adverse effect on daytime deer activity.

temperature and might sometimes override the influence of temperature on deer movement. However, unless temperature matches a whitetail's comfort zone, movement will halt during daylight hours.

To experience optimal deer activity during hunting season at the 40th to 45th parallel north , I've found that daytime air temperatures should not exceed 55 degrees. On the other hand, there is a low end to a whitetail's comfort zone. At the same latitudes, temperatures below 20 degrees will generally curtail activity unless the chase phase of the rut is full blown. An exception to this occurrs if there have been several days of extreme heat or cold. Then, any snap as little as 10 degrees cooler or warmer will trigger movement. But as a rule, I've found that most deer activity occurs when temperatures are in the normal range for a particular area in the North. The South is a different story.

In places like Texas, which has a different subspecies of deer than the North, whitetails operate under an entirely different comfort zone. It's not uncommon to see good deer movement in southern Texas brush country when temperatures are in the 80s, providing the rut is on and a storm isn't raging. Whitetails in this environment have

Movements of Deer in Response to Hunting Pressure

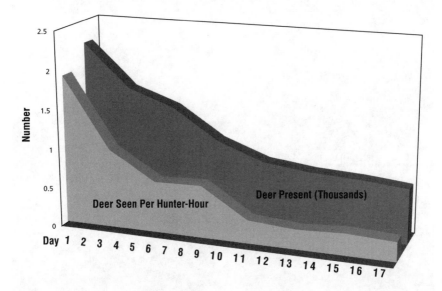

Chart showing what hunting pressure does to deer activity. With hunters in the woods, deer move less during daylight hours.

shorter hair and can tolerate heat better.

Whitetails in the northern bush of Canada — at the 52nd parallel north— seem to have a comfort zone about 10 degrees lower than whitetails found in the United States. After hunting big Saskatchewan whitetails for several years, I have found that their comfort zone ranges from about 15 to 45 degrees during November.

When the mercury rises above or below a whitetail's comfort zone, deer generally shut down and move little on their own, unless a storm front is approaching.

Human Pressure: Region of the Country

In most parts of the country, the rutting moon period occurs during archery season, so human pressure is not as great as during firearms season. However, in more populated areas, human pressure can pose a problem. Whitetails quickly learn that darkness is quieter, less threatening and has fewer people.

The graph that accompanies this chapter shows what happens to deer sightings when hunters invade a whitetail's domain. Remember

In areas where gang-hunting is legal, whitetails quickly become nocturnal.

that it's not just hunters that suppress daytime activity. The presence of any human puts whitetails on red alert. This can mean hikers, bird-watchers or bow-hunters. So, if a hunting area experiences human activity higher than that found during nonhunting months, it is likely that deer will confine their movements to nighttime.

Location and the amount of human pressure can affect daytime deer sightings tremendously. Many urban areas have high deer populations, but unless landowners are feeding deer, they seldom see them. Human noises, whether from automobiles, sirens or children playing, keep deer hunkered down and out of sight until the safety of darkness. This is especially true with mature bucks. Human pressure can and does suppress daytime deer activity.

Skewed Adult Doe to Buck Ratio

Volumes have been written on how high adult doe-to-buck ratios shut down the rut. If you hunt an area that has more than four or five adult does for every antlered buck, the rut will be light, with little

When there are more than four adult does for every antlered buck, rutting activity will be much less intense than in herds with a 1-1 ratio.

chasing, rubbing and scraping. If you hunt an area where the ratio is three adult does to every antlered buck, the rut should have a fair amount of visible rutting activity. If the ratio is 1-to-1 or two adult does for every buck, rutting activity — in the form of chasing, fighting, rubbing and scraping — will be outstanding. And yes, a few places in North America do have more antlered bucks than adult does. In these areas, the rut tends to be unbelievable, beyond imagination.

Through the years, I've photographed and hunted areas that contain the adult doe-to-buck ratios I've described. It's been quite an education, and I've learned that whatever the adult doe-to-buck ratio, so goes the rut. It's that simple.

The bottom line is that without competition, there is no need for bucks to go ballistic. Poor ratios suppress rutting activity, night or day, especially in areas where 70 percent to 90 percent of the buck harvest is comprised of yearlings. This is particularly evident in states where the doe population has been protected at the expense of

Deer gravitate to preferable food sources. Therefore, if the food source in your area goes bust, don't expect much deer activity.

Legal baiting can change the complexity of the rut immensely. When deer gravitate to a certain food, many of their natural habits change.

antlered bucks. When too much pressure is put on bucks, all aspects of the whitetail world suffer, especially rutting behavior.

Another thing that lessens the intensity of rutting activity is the absence of mature bucks. In areas where a deer population has adequate numbers of mature bucks, the rut's intensity is greater in every aspect, from scraping to breeding.

So, if you don't see the rut as predicted, there is a good chance it's because of poor adult doe-to-buck ratios and a lack of mature bucks.

Food Sources

If you want to see the rut's chemistry change, look no farther than food sources. The rut and its sequence will happen; you just won't see it unless you have good food sources to lure does.

This occurs regularly in my area because of the cyclical nature of the acorn crop. When there is a good acorn crop, deer will be where acorns are falling. Because does are present, bucks will be nearby. When the rut begins, scraping, rubbing, fighting and breeding will be at the hunter's doorstep. If the mast goes bust the next year, the hunter who thought he was in whitetail heaven the year before

Rut suppressors are cumulative. If too many are present, bucks will chase, scrape, rub and breed only at night during the rutting moon.

suddenly finds himself in a predicament because he's not seeing the rut he saw last year. Because of this, he thinks, "This year was crazy. I never did see the rut as predicted." In reality, it boils down to this: No food, few deer. Few deer, little or no visible rut.

Whitetails are driven by food, so they'll do what is necessary to find proper nutrition. This often means they'll change their range to survive. In farm country, this might mean only a two- to three-mile shift. But in big timber country, it is often greater. Unfortunately, hunters seldom have the freedom to shift with deer.

If you are skeptical, pay close attention to how food sources contribute to the rut's complexity. In some areas, the impact can be profound. If your hunting area doesn't have a good food source come fall, the best advice I can give is to move where deer are feeding. If you don't, you will probably miss the excitement when the rutting moon arrives.

It's a sure bet that in many areas where baiting is legal, he who has the biggest bait pile wins.

Baiting

If you want to open a can of worms, just mention baiting to hunters. It's a hot topic where it's practiced. Baiting can suppress the rut just like the boom and bust of natural food sources. It's a sure bet that in many areas where baiting is legal, he who has the biggest bait pile wins. Baiting can change the face of the rut when deer are lured off a property that doesn't bait and onto another that does. This is one reason why there are so many high-fenced operations in Texas. With legal baiting, Texas landowners can't keep deer on their property unless they bait. So, as a last resort, landowners fence their ranches to stop deer from moving to surrounding properties.

If baiting is legal where you hunt and you choose not to bait, don't be surprised if your neighbors see more rutting behavior than you.

CHAPTER 13

Observations of an Eastern Moon-Watcher, 1998

I've been writing about the rutting moon for several years. In the October 1998 issue of *Deer & Deer Hunting,* I predicted the 1998 whitetail breeding period would be traditional, like what hunters were always told it would be. In 1998, the rutting moon was Nov. 4. From research, I knew the bucks' seeking and chasing phase would kick in about Nov. 2. From experience, I also believed breeding would begin about Nov. 11 and remain full-blown until about Nov. 25. All the data wasn't in at press time, but I knew about 80 percent — rather than the typical 70 percent — of the research does were bred during the 14-day breeding window Laroche and I predicted.

Fall 1998 was the first season in 15 years that I didn't take a whitetail hunting trip to another part of America. I did this so I could collect rutting data from other breeders, and monitor what was happening with wild deer and enclosure deer at my farm. I also had to converse regularly with Saskatchewan outfitter Bentley Brown. We planned to keep diaries to monitor what was occurring in the East and West. Although I dearly missed hunting elsewhere, I'm glad I opted to stay home and collect data. It was worth the sacrifice.

My New York Experience

Our farm set-up is unique. My family and I live on a 213-acre western New York farm we've converted into a wildlife sanctuary/whitetail-research facility. We have 10 whitetails inside a 35-acre high-fenced enclosure. In Fall 1998, the population included four mature bucks, one yearling buck, four adult does, two buck fawns and one doe fawn. The most deer I keep in the facility after Dec. 15 is 11, and I sell excess deer to other breeders. I use the enclosure solely for research, and there's no hunting allowed inside. I mention this to eliminate confusion. I hunt only on the parts of our farm or other areas where deer are wild and free-roaming.

1998 was a typical year for pre-rut behavior. Deer fed heavily in apples and field crops throughout September and October.

Also, some surrounding landowners and I practice quality deer management, so the free-ranging population on my farm includes several mature bucks. This, coupled with the enclosure, makes an interesting laboratory.

Before October 1998, Brown and I discussed how we would catalog our observations. We decided to make things simple, and agreed to merely chronicle the weather, number of deer seen and types of rutting activity observed.

Because Saskatchewan's season opened Nov. 2, Brown would start his diary later than mine. Therefore, I'll summarize my findings for the last 15 days of October '98.

Oct. 15 to Nov. 1

The weather was typical for this period, although maybe drier than normal. Usually, nights were in the 30s, with daytime temperatures ranging from the high 40s to the low 60s. Because of this, daytime activity wasn't great inside or outside the enclosure. From Oct. 20 to 22, I hunted six times without seeing a buck outside the enclosure. However, the nighttime scraping activity of wild deer increased signifi-

As October ended, rubbing activity increased considerably.

From the last week of October through the first 10 days of November, scraping was as intense as I've ever seen on our farm.

Thanks to an active quality deer management program in our area, I found many rubs like this during Fall 1998.

cantly about Oct. 20, especially in natural travel corridors. From Oct. 15 to Nov. 1, daytime sightings of wild does were high, but wild buck sightings were almost nonexistent.

Nov. 2 to 4

On Nov. 2 and 3, the hunter's moon shone almost full. During darkness, air temperatures dipped into the 30s, and daytime temperatures were in the 40s and low 50s. Things began clicking in the woods.

On the morning of Nov. 4, I had a close encounter with a 130-class 9-pointer. Ten minutes before he appeared, six does and fawns passed my stand. When I saw the buck cruising through the woods with his nose to the ground, I grunted three times to stop him. He stopped and came toward me. Unfortunately, he hung up 20 yards from me and scanned the woods. With my bow ready for full draw, the chess match began. The wind was perfect, and I knew he'd eventually step into the nearby shooting lane. However, it was not meant to be. The wind suddenly shifted — the only time it did all morning. I felt it cooling the back of my neck, and I knew the buck would wind me in seconds. When he got a snout full of my scent, he snorted, wheeled and ran off

Late in the day Nov. 12, I rattled in and killed this beautiful buck while hunting an active scrape line. To date, it's the best buck I've arrowed on our farm.

where he came from.

After an hour of silence and no deer sightings — an hour of constantly thinking what might have been — I climbed down to check the enclosure deer. First, I walked the perimeter fence. I found six paw-beds in a 400-yard stretch. From the sign, I knew wild bucks had been aggressively interacting with bucks inside the enclosure at night. Things were heating up. On average, I was seeing six bucks per day outside the enclosure.

Nov. 5 to 6
On Nov. 5, the rut switch was thrown. The day dawned overcast and windless. It was cold — 40 to 45 degrees — and remained overcast and windless.

It stayed cloud-covered at night Nov. 5 and 6, and scraping, rubbing and chasing were in full throttle. On Nov. 6, I saw 10 bucks outside the enclosure.

Nov. 7 to 9
Weather conditions and deer activity were identical to Nov. 5 and 6.

On Nov. 7, I decided to scout a section of the farm I hadn't hunted. In one 300-yard-long travel corridor, I counted 21 scrapes. It was incredible.

From Nov. 5 through 9, bucks were moving, and chasing was intense. During this time, I passed up five yearling and 2½-year-old bucks. Several times, I had other bucks within 50 yards of my stands, but I couldn't coax them within 20 yards, which was the shooting range I'd set.

Inside the enclosure, adult bucks were increasing scraping, rubbing and chasing. Their behavior mirrored what was occurring in the wild population.

On Nov. 7, I decided to scout a section of the farm I hadn't hunted. In one 300-yard-long travel corridor, I counted 21 scrapes. I had never found so much rutting sign on our farm. It was incredible. I immediately hung a stand overlooking three of the scrapes and began hunting. During this period, I averaged six buck sightings per day outside the enclosure.

Nov. 10 to 12

After days of overcast skies, the sun shown again. Temperatures ranged from the low 30s to low 50s. Midmorning to midafternoon winds were higher than normal, making hunting difficult during the two hours after sunrise and the two hours before sunset. On stand the morning of Nov. 10, I had a close encounter with one of the mature bucks that was ranging several nearby farms. Unfortunately, he was chasing a doe back and forth through the woods, and his antics prohibited me from taking a shot. I'm not sure how many points he had, but he was big.

From Nov. 10 through 12, I passed up several bucks as they came to freshen scrapes. Scraping was intense almost everywhere I looked.

On Nov. 12, with 45 minutes of hunting remaining on a clear, cold day, I rattled in and killed the biggest archery buck of my career seconds after he worked a scrape in front of me.

That night, I called Dave Buckley of West Valley, N.Y. Dave is retired and one of the best whitetail hunters I've met. I knew he'd been

Trying to monitor wild deer outside the enclosure would soon be difficult because gun season would start.

hunting his farm every day, and I wanted to know what he'd been seeing. Although we live more than 100 miles apart, our observations were almost identical. We agreed we were seeing a traditional, intense rut. I was seeing an average of five bucks per day outside the enclosure.

Nov. 13 to 15

These were the last two days of New York's archery season. Trying to monitor wild deer outside the enclosure would soon be difficult because gun season would start. With New York's run-and-gun mentality, I knew most bucks would become nocturnal by the third day of shotgun season.

With my archery season finished, I began scouting the farm. I found scrapes everywhere, but less than half appeared to be fresh. Could breeding be starting? On the afternoon of Nov. 13, my first adult research doe was bred. One down, three to go. Actually, I had noticed the bucks were paying close attention to her the day before. I knew she was close, and I was ready to observe it.

On Nov. 14, I witnessed a spectacular chase while scouting the northern end of our farm. For nearly 15 minutes, I stood motionless beside a big beech tree, and watched a 120-class 8-pointer try to cut a hot doe from a group of five does and fawns. He was persistent, and she was resistant, which made the experience special.

After scouting Nov. 15, I concluded that breeding had kicked into high gear. Why? Very few scrapes had been worked. This is a clear sign the rut phase was changing from chasing to breeding. Because I didn't hunt mornings or evenings, my buck sightings decreased to an average of three per day outside the enclosure.

Nov. 16 to 18

On Nov. 16, shotgun season began. The temperature was about 35 degrees, and the day was windless and partially overcast. By 10 a.m., the weather had worsened, and rain began to fall. As with every gun-

By Nov. 14, many of the scrapes on our farm had gone cold, indicating that breeding had begun.

hunt opener, I tried to note when I heard the first shot. That morning, it was 6:40 a.m., which was too early for me to see movement. At 7:15 a.m., a 5-pointer cruised by my stand with his nose to the ground. He didn't have a clue I was in the area as he smelled his way past at 20 yards. Does do those things to bucks. At 8 a.m., I used my pocket radio to contact one of my caretakers inside the deer enclosure. I wanted to know what was going on.

"Jeremy, what's happening?" I said.

"Not much on this end," he replied. "The bucks are all bedded, and I don't know where the does are. They must be in some other part of the enclosure. About a half-hour ago, I saw does running around outside the enclosure. I don't know if they were running from hunters or a buck."

"OK, I'll touch base with you in an hour," I said.

The instant I put down the radio, I saw a doe running at my stand with a big buck in tow. For the next couple of minutes, he chased her around the stand before disappearing. Several times, I could have shot him, but I never touched the safety. If I hadn't killed a beautiful archery buck, I might have been tempted. I stopped counting shots at 85,

By the time the first week in December rolled around and the post-rut moon arrived, bucks were reverting to bachelor-group behavior. It marked the end of another glorious season.

and by afternoon the woods was dead. By the end of the day, I had seen 13 does and five bucks, including three I could have killed.

The next two days, I hunted the spruce funnel where I killed my archery buck. Despite opening day's noisy disruption, deer activity was high. With clear, cold temperatures, I passed up four bucks as they cruised the thick spruce plantation looking for does. At least all the does were not in estrus yet. On Nov. 17, my second research doe was bred. Two down, two to go.

Nov. 19 to 30

With shotgun season going full bore, trying to monitor wild deer behavior was difficult — but not impossible. On Nov. 20, I returned to the spruce funnel because deer activity there was high. The day dawned clear and frosty, with temperatures in the high 20s. During the morning, I saw 10 does and fawns and two yearling bucks, but no shooters.

My son, Aaron, had yet to hunt during gun season because of his college schedule. When he got home at midday, I shared my morning's

The last doe was bred Nov. 30. With that,
the 1998 rut ended abruptly.
However, from my observations,
it was as intense as any rut I've seen.

experiences, and told him he'd better get to our favorite spruce stand quickly. He did, and late in the day killed a beautiful 2½-year-old 8-pointer as it cruised through the funnel. The buck's behavior indicated he was on the move looking for does.

Despite the gun-season mortality, I still encountered bucks. However, as the days passed, I observed less rutting behavior for two reasons. First, daytime temperatures soared into the high 60s. Also, with estrous does covering little ground, buck activity was becoming nonexistent as the end of November approached.

However, inside the research facility, the interaction between bucks and the two does that hadn't yet been bred was intense. Although scraping had decreased, aggressive rubbing, chasing and vocalizations were in high gear as the four adult bucks jockeyed for the remaining does. On Nov. 21, the third research doe was bred. Only a yearling remained. She was bred Nov. 30. With that, the 1998 rut ended abruptly. It concluded as quickly as it had started Nov. 3. However, from my observations, it was as intense as any rut I've seen.

In the next chapter, I'll share Brown's 1998 observations, and conclude the chapter with my analysis of conclusions from East and West.

CHAPTER 14

Observations from the West, 1998

November in Saskatchewan can be a human endurance test. I've hunted this province several times, and the weather took me to the limit almost every time. It's no place for hunters who dislike snow and cold. However, if you want to hunt some of the continent's biggest whitetails, Saskatchewan is the place.

I began hunting Saskatchewan whitetails in 1992. During my first trip, I hooked up with an outfitter who supposedly knew how to hunt whitetails. It turned out he didn't. A week after I returned from that trip, I headed back. The second time, I hunted with Bentley Brown of Turtleford, Saskatchewan, and I've been hunting with him since. Through the years, I've hunted with many outfitters, some of whom are known as the best. However, Brown is the best outfitter I've hunted with. He knows whitetails in and out, and is as hard a worker as I've seen. Simply put, he knows how to hunt whitetails.

This chapter is a continuation of Chapter 13 and describes what occurred in a part of Saskatchewan during November 1998. It also shows the relationship between different latitudes. The observations I discussed in the previous chapter happened at the 42nd parallel north. Brown's observations occurred at the 52nd parallel north. Some folks believe such a latitudinal shift can affect Laroche's and my hypothesis about the breeding dates of Northern whitetails.

New York and Saskatchewan differ greatly in geography and deer-herd chemistry. Saskatchewan has fewer deer but a much better buck-to-adult-doe ratio than New York. Also, Brown's hunting area has almost no agriculture, and is what many consider unbroken wilderness. Western New York is farm country. Despite this, seven years of comparisons have convinced me the regions have few differences in the breeding window for whitetails.

Since 1996, Brown and I have shared information regarding whitetail movement as it relates to the moon. Last summer, I asked him to keep detailed notes about what he and his hunters saw during November 1998. As you'll see, we found many parallels between our experiences, although we live more than 2,000 miles apart.

Rutting behavior in Saskatchewan mirrored that of New York during 1998.

During our conversations late last summer, I told Brown to look closely at his 1992 and 1995 records, because the rutting moon occurred Nov. 9 and Nov. 5, respectively, those years. I hunted with Brown in 1992 and knew it was one of his best years — especially the season's second week and Thanksgiving week. Could 1998 provide a repeat? I told Brown in early October that I believed strongly it would. I also told him that if 1998 mirrored 1995 — a three-peat — we'd have enough data to predict his future, or at least have a good idea about any year's prospects based on when the rutting moon occurred.

Week 1: Nov. 2 to 7

The week's weather was consistent, featuring medium-overcast conditions and daytime temperatures of about 20 to 35. During the week, each of the six hunters in camp had opportunities to kill deer. By the week's end, three had killed respectable bucks. They drew first blood on the second day, Nov. 3. The best deer activity occurred Nov. 5. Activity was high all week, but especially during Nov. 5, 6 and 7. Several hunters saw bucks chasing. Even before the first day of hunting, Brown and his guides observed heavy scraping and rubbing. On average, each hunter saw 2.1 bucks per day.

From right,   Bentley Brown, Jim Damon of Oklahoma and I look at a map after I killed a beautiful Saskatchewan buck.

Week 2: Nov. 9 to 13

Saskatchewan doesn't allow hunting on Sundays, so the second group, which had six hunters, hit the woods Nov. 9. Like the first week, conditions were overcast, with daytime temperatures ranging from 20 to 28. As expected, this group saw great action all week, including an assortment of rutting behavior. On Nov. 9 and 10, buck sightings were particularly high. By dusk Nov. 10, three big bucks hung on the pole.

"The 10th turned out to be one of the best days all season," Brown said.

All the hunters killed bucks, and overall action and sightings were very good. During the week, hunters and guides saw rubs and scrapes everywhere. On average, each hunter saw about three bucks per day.

Week 3: Nov. 16 to 20

This was the coldest week, featuring overcast to partly cloudy conditions. Daytime temperatures ranged from 7 to 20 the first five days before warming to 28 the last day. By week's end, four of the six hunters had scored, and all had chances to kill trophy bucks. Throughout the

Bentley Brown photo

Norm Amos of New York killed this 167-inch buck with Brown on Nov. 3, 1998, the second day of Saskatchewan's deer season.

week, hunters and guides found new scrapes and rubs, and rutting activity was intense. On average, each hunter saw 2.46 bucks per day.

Week 4:
Nov. 23 to 28

Conditions varied from clear to partly cloudy, to overcast and snowing. Daytime temperatures ranged from 20 to 32. From a hunting standpoint, it was a short week. All six hunters killed bucks in the 150- to 170-inch range by Thursday. Buck activity on Nov. 23 and 24 was very high, especially on Nov. 23, when hunters saw 26 bucks, the most of any

Scraping activity was high during Saskatchewan's deer season.

day during the season. Nov. 23 was the first clear day after several overcast days, which might have contributed to buck movement. According to Brown, Nov. 24 was the second-best day of the season for buck sightings. On Nov. 28, with all the hunters tagged out, Brown and his guides scouted. During the day, they saw the highest buck activity of the year. Unfortunately, they had no hunters in the field. On average, each hunter saw 4.5 bucks per day. Overall, this was the best week of the season.

Week 5: Nov. 30 to Dec. 5

Hunting conditions ranged from clear to overcast skies with snow, and daytime temperatures were in the high 20s. Buck activity didn't slow much from the previous week, and two of the four hunters killed trophy bucks the first day. By the third day, all the hunters had killed respectable bucks. Bucks seemed to be moving, and hunters saw yearling bucks chasing does. On average, each hunter saw 3.7 bucks per day.

Brown's hunters kill many outstanding bucks each year.

Analysis of East and West

An analysis of what happened in New York and Saskatchewan reveals numerous similarities. In each location, chasing was high during and after the rutting moon. Each area saw great deer movement Nov. 5, the day after the rutting moon.

The heavy buck activity I saw Nov. 9 through 12 was mirrored in Saskatchewan. I saw more bucks than Brown's hunters, but my hunting area has more than twice as many deer. During Brown's scouting the first week of November, he found lots of rubbing and scraping. In the previous chapter, I also mentioned the high amount of scraping I found Nov. 7. Was this coincidence? I don't think so. The rutting moon triggered most of this.

There were some interesting parallels between what Brown and I witnessed during mid-November. Although we saw buck activity, it wasn't as intense as it had been Nov. 1 through 14. Breeding had blossomed, and bucks weren't roaming as much.

Unfortunately, it's difficult for me to make more accurate comparisons for Nov. 23 through 28, because our gun season was into its second week. However, the buck/doe interaction I saw and cataloged at my research facility was almost identical to what Brown saw in his wild

I rattled in this 162-inch Saskatchewan buck during the hunter's moon period in 1993.

population.

The comparison of New York and Saskatchewan ended Nov. 30, because my last research doe was bred that day. That provoked intense chaos in the research facility, despite 70-degree temperatures. It was simply too hot the rest of the week to see daytime deer activity in New York. However, what I saw Nov. 30 was, again, consistent with what Brown saw.

An Overview

After several years of hunting with Brown, I strongly believed rutting activity in Saskatchewan was similar to that in western New York. I also believed it varied somewhat each year. It wasn't until I asked Brown to record everything he and his hunters saw that my original beliefs were confirmed. Now, it's clear to me the rutting moon has a tremendous influence on buck activity across North America. No doubt, some people will be skeptical, even after reading chapters 13 and 14. Because one year of documentation isn't enough, I'll provide further evidence.

In 1996, the rutting moon occurred Oct. 26. I surprised Brown that year when I told him I wanted to hunt his first week. Based on the

This is my best whitetail to date. I killed this 175-inch buck while hunting with Brown in 1994.

rutting moon, I believed that would be the best week. Before I was involved in moon research, I had always wanted to hunt the second or third week.

"Are you sure you know what you're doing?" Brown asked. "Why don't you come the second week in November? That's always better than the first week."

"Well, I'm working on something I feel strongly about, and I think the full moon has an influence on when the rut kicks in," I said. "With an Oct. 26 rutting moon, I believe your opening week will be great."

"OK, if you say so," he said. "Come then if you want."

So, Jim Damon of Oklahoma, a *Deer & Deer Hunting* sweepstakes winner, and I hunted with Brown the first week in November. The rest is history. Buck activity was unusually good — according to Brown— and Damon and I each killed 160-class bucks. All six hunters scored, and we finished hunting by the fifth day. Brown had never filled up so fast during opening week. This was more than coincidence, at least in my opinion. I'd been collecting breeding data for almost two years, and my observations of the rutting moon's influence caused me to change my thinking in 1996 — and every year since.

In 1999, the rutting moon occurred Oct. 24, which was identical to 1996. Whether you're in New York or Saskatchewan, the end of October and first week in November should provide great opportunities in years like these. As in 1998, Brown and I planned to compare notes in 1999 to better determine what the rutting moon has to offer.

To contact Brown, write to Box 475, Turtleford, Sask., Canada S0M 2Y0, or call him at (306) 845-2444.

CHAPTER 15

Through the Hunter's Eye: Another Perspective

Now and then, I encounter someone who has what I call "a Ph.D. in life." This has nothing to do with an advanced degree from a university. It's earned the hard way, through the school of hard knocks, by mastering a subject or an aspect of life better than most people. In my life, I've met or heard of many with talents not learned in a traditional classroom. Most of these people turned out to be fascinating. Derrick Woodlen, of Ringgold, Ga., is such a person. Woodlen is not a biologist, writer or noted deer hunter. However, he's certainly one of the most detailed whitetail hunters I've heard of.

In the October 1998 issue of *Deer & Deer Hunting,* Woodland presented an article entitled "The Best Times To Hunt: One Man's Perspective." The piece was powerful, and revealed much about when deer can be expected to move. Overall, I believe the piece was on target concerning the movements of white-tailed deer in autumn and early winter. For 25 years, Woodlen documented every deer he saw while scouting and hunting in Alabama, Georgia and Tennessee. During those two and a half decades, he recorded the time, weather conditions, rutting activity, feeding habits, moon phases and countless other pieces of information. It was during the computing and calculating process that several patterns emerged.

The charts that accompany this chapter are a result of Woodlen's work. As a person who's been observing, photographing, hunting and raising whitetails for almost 40 years, I'm often skeptical when I see what "mere" hunters have put together. However, that is not the case here. I've looked at Woodlen's data closely, comparing it to what I've learned after a lifetime with whitetails, and I've found it to be accurate.

When Woodlen started collecting data in 1972, one of his goals was to help hunters better understand the whitetail. I think he has accomplished this, and I'm sure you will think so, too, after reading and studying the charts that accompany the text. If there ever was a deer hunting article tailor-made to complement a hunter education class,

Deer Movement in Relation to the Wind

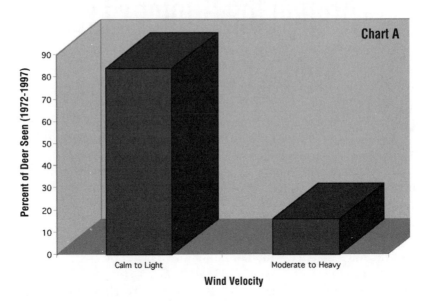

As documented more than 20 years ago by reader surveys in **Deer & Deer Hunting,** *deer activity generally decreases as wind speed increases. Derrick Woodlen, a deer-hunting fanatic from Georgia, found deer activity was greatest when winds were calm to light. Of the thousands of deer he has documented, 84 percent were seen during these conditions. However, Woodlen saw some deer activity — 16 percent of his sightings — when winds were moderate to heavy. According to previous* **D&DH** *research, the dividing line seems to be about 15 mph. Deer tend to group and become nervous in high winds. During cold weather, high winds make deer seek shelter on the lee slopes of hills and in dense coniferous woodlands. Conifer stands can reduce winds by 75 percent.*

this is it.

When looking at the charts, remember that nothing is absolute when it comes to whitetails. So at best, what follows describes what can be expected to happen rather than what will happen.

Wind: Chart A

Chart A shows what can happen during varying wind conditions. According to Woodlen's research, the best time to hunt is with calm to light northwest winds. In Woodlen's region, this is probably sound advice. However, I believe it is site specific. In my experience, different parts of North America have different prevailing winds. For example, in Saskatchewan a northern wind is most common. In my home

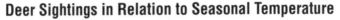

Deer Sightings in Relation to Seasonal Temperature

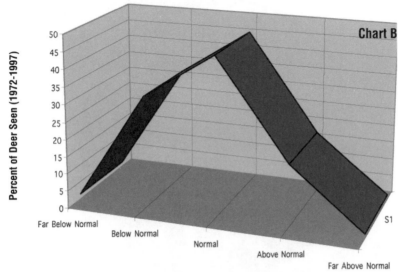

Daily Thermometer Readings Compared to Regional Averages

The best chances of seeing deer occur when temperatures are at or slightly below seasonal averages. In fact, of all the deer Woodlen has seen, more than 77 percent were spotted during this type of weather. Of all the deer he observed, just 1.5 percent were seen when temperatures were far below normal, and only 1.7 percent were seen when temperatures were far above normal. Deer sightings were average — 18 percent of the total seen during the 25-year study — when the mercury was slightly above normal. Overall, however, 46 percent of the deer Woodlen observed were seen when temperatures were normal for his hunting area in Georgia.

state of New York, the prevailing wind is from the southwest. Remember calm or light winds — not direction — are what cause greater deer movement.

Woodlen also debunks a common belief about buck movements. He wrote: "How often have you read or heard that a buck will always travel with his nose into the wind? Well, since 1972, I've seen just as many bucks walking with the wind as I've seen walking into it."

I agree. In my experience, a rut-crazed buck goes where he wants and usually does what he must to distinguish odors.

Temperature: Chart B

I've written about air temperature numerous times in the past 20

Deer Movement in Relation to Sky Conditions

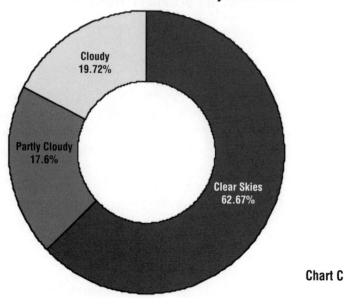

Cloudy
19.72%

Partly Cloudy
17.6%

Clear Skies
62.67%

Chart C

Not including other factors, such as the rut, temperature changes and feeding activity, days with clear skies ranked far above other sky conditions when it comes to seeing deer. By a whopping 3-to-1 margin, Woodlen documented the most deer activity on clear days. On many occasions in autumn, clear skies can be associated with cold fronts, which typically bring low relative humidity and light winds. Combined, these conditions almost always lead to good deer activity, Woodlen found.

years, and I consider it a critical part of a whitetail's chemistry. It can directly influence when deer move, bed and feed. I often refer to it as the "fur factor" because if temperatures are not right, deer will not move. Woodlen's Chart B is a reminder that whitetails have a comfort zone.

A deer's comfort zone varies, depending on location. Whitetails have adapted to every region of the country, so it's important to know what the normal temperature is for your hunting area.

"Deer activity increases after cold snaps," Woodlen said. "For example, when temperatures are extremely cold and then it begins to warm up, deer activity increases. The same is true when a long stretch of hot weather is suddenly replaced by cool weather."

So, watch the temperature.

Sky Conditions: Chart C

In his *D&DH* article Woodlen said, "When comparing clear days to days with any type of cloud cover, clear days prove to be the most productive for seeing deer on the move. Many times, clear skies can be associated with cool fronts, bringing in cooler temperatures, low relative humidity, and calm to light winds. This has proven to be a good time for deer movement."

I've found that clear days preceding and following a storm front are excellent times to see deer on moving, providing temperatures are normal for the time of year. On clear days before a storm front moves in — signified by rapidly falling barometric pressure — deer rush to get one more meal before nasty weather arrives. Then, after the storm front passes — rising barometric pressure — deer catch up on the prime feeding times they skipped when conditions were miserable.

Don't rule out overcast days during the peak of

Time of Day Deer Were Seen

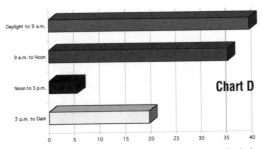

Chart D

Percent of Deer Seen During Each Time Period

As evidenced above, mornings are the best time to see deer. Of all the deer Woodlen saw while hunting and scouting since 1972, 39.56 percent appeared between daylight and 9 a.m. The second time period — 9 a.m. to noon — ranked a close second at 35.25 percent. The worst time to see deer was from noon to 3 p.m.

Chart E, below, documents buck activity. Most bucks were seen early in the morning, 40.17 percent, followed by the time period of 9 a.m. to noon, 39.39 percent. Overall, buck activity drops sharply after noon — 8 percent of the deer seen between noon and 3 p.m. were bucks — before picking up again from 3 p.m. to dark, 13.39 percent. This chart shows that hunters who stay on their stands longer in the morning have good chances of seeing more bucks.

Time of Day Bucks Were Seen

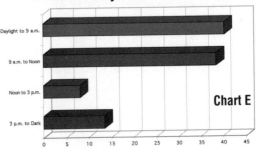

Chart E

Percent of Deer Seen that were Bucks

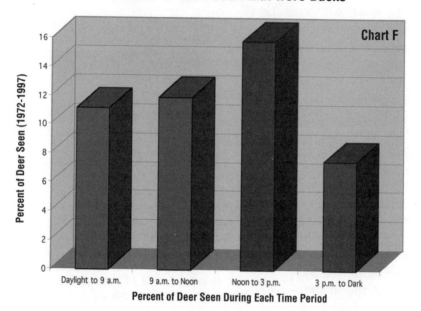

Percent of Deer Seen that were Bucks

Chart F

Percent of Deer Seen (1972-1997)

Daylight to 9 a.m.   9 a.m. to Noon   Noon to 3 p.m.   3 p.m. to Dark

Percent of Deer Seen During Each Time Period

Although Woodlen doesn't see many deer between noon and 3 p.m., a higher percentage of these deer are bucks, when compared to other time periods. Of the deer he's seen in the afternoon since 1972, 15.78 percent were bucks. Of the deer he's seen from 9 a.m. to noon, 11.94 percent were bucks. Bucks also made up 11.13 percent of deer seen from daylight to 9 a.m. The time period of 3 p.m. to dark ranked low. Only 7.5 percent of deer seen were bucks.

the rut's chase phase. In the North, I've found that if it's overcast with light to no wind and the temperature is near freezing during chasing time, bucks are often on the fly. Even if there is just a little snow spitting, things can get interesting in the woods. Woodlen's information on this is excellent, but remember there are always exceptions.

Time of Day: Charts D, E & F

Charts D and E can offer a lot of information to novice and seasoned hunters. I only wish someone had provided me with this information when I started deer hunting nearly four decades ago. It's obvious some of Woodlen's data is time specific. It probably was taken during archery season, because when firearms season begins, deer become nocturnal, and daytime activity nearly ceases.

"Hunters can toss out all data on the best times to see deer if they allow a buck to pattern their movements," Woodlen said. "If you enter

The best chances of seeing deer occur when temperatures are at or slightly below seasonal averages.

Deer Seen in Each Moon Phase

Chart G

After documenting all deer sightings during hunting and scouting trips since 1972, Woodlen concluded no moon phase is head-and-shoulders above another for overall deer activity, as indicated in Chart G, above. However, his data indicates the full-moon phase holds a slight edge over the first quarter, followed by the new moon and last quarter. Significant activity trends surface, however, when breaking down this information into buck-only activity, as seen in Chart H, below. Here, Woodlen discovered buck activity was greatest on days of the full-moon phase. Of the deer he saw during full moons, nearly 32 percent were bucks. However, he was least likely to see buck activity on days when the moon was in its first quarter. Of the deer he saw those days, only 20 percent were bucks.

Bucks Seen in Each Moon Phase

Chart H

the woods a little before daylight, come out at 11 a.m., head back at 4 p.m., and stay until dark, deer will quickly recognize your hunting pattern. In turn, deer will move when you're not there. Most seasoned hunters I know plan accordingly, hunt at midday and enjoy tremendous success."

My records show that through the years, I've had some deviation from Chart E. I've found that in the pre-rut, I see the most buck activity from 3 p.m. until dark. However, after the seeking, chasing and breeding phases of the rut kick in, my buck sighting data coincides with Woodlen's.

Chart F provides interesting information. Unfortunately, I don't have data from free-roaming deer to compare with Woodlen's findings. However, I know that in confined herds, within large high-fenced operations, deer are accustomed to man. I've seen above-average buck movement in the noon to 3 p.m. time frame. While hunting Saskatchewan on Nov. 14, 1994, I killed my biggest buck ever

Woodlen discovered good buck activity during days of the full-moon phase. Of the deer he observed between daylight and 9 a.m., 53.12 percent were bucks. Bucks moved throughout the day, but the percentage decreased rapidly after 9 a.m. The author discovered an interesting trend during days of the last-quarter moon phase. As with the full moon, buck activity was greatest in the morning. Of deer seen between 9 a.m. and noon, 39.13 percent were bucks.

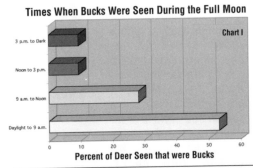

Times When Bucks Were Seen During the Full Moon

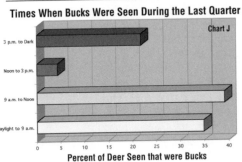

Times When Bucks Were Seen During the Last Quarter

(175 B&C) when he cruised by my tree stand alone at 1:25 p.m.

The Moon's Influence: Charts G-L

Chart G shows Woodlen's findings on deer movement during various moon phases. This data is similar to other research, and nearly mirrors Hofacker's 1977-1981 work. However, unlike Hofacker's study, Woodlen went one step further and showed the percentage of bucks seen in each moon phase — Chart H.

Charts I, J, K and L are more specific, and show the times of buck sightings during the four moon phases. I couldn't agree more with Chart I, especially during the rutting moon and last quarter — three-quarters waning — moon.

After 25 years of collecting data, Woodlen found that his best hunting scenario is to be in his favorite deer stand on a clear, frosty morning during a full moon period. This is opposite of what he and I were taught while growing up, but years of in-the-field work have taught us that magical things happen when weather conditions and the full moon come together in harmony.

After years of observing whitetails, I've found that when a full moon is rising at the same time the sun is setting — or vice versa — deer activity will be high if suppressors are minimal.

The author's observations during days of the new moon followed the pattern of his data for the first-quarter phase. However, buck movement was more pronounced from 9 a.m. to noon. Of the deer seen during that period, 44 percent were bucks. Deer activity was stable during the moon's first-quarter phase. Again, buck activity was best during the morning — 42.85 percent of deer seen between 9 a.m. and noon were bucks. As you can see, afternoon buck activity was flat.

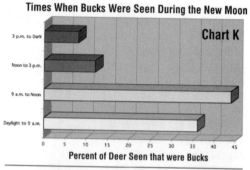

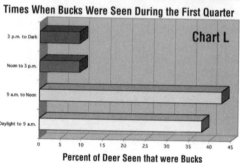

The Rut: Charts M & N

In Chart M, Woodlen makes the following observation: "I have found that deer movement is predictable as the hunting season progresses. Sightings increase steadily as the early season gives way to the pre-rut, and the pre-rut transforms into the rut. In addition, I've found that deer activity drastically falls immediately after the rut's peak, and it is reduced more as the post-rut wanes. Secondary rut activity is also minimal, at best.

"In Chart M, you will see the percentages of deer I observed at various times of the hunting seasons. More than 25 percent were seen during the rut's peak. Because rutting activity varies by region, you will have to translate this information to your region."

I think Woodlen knows why deer activity decreases drastically after the rut's peak even though he doesn't say so. As I've pointed out in other chapters, rutting activity, like scraping, crashes when full-blown breeding begins. This is a classic indicator that rutting behavior will be decreasing.

Woodland concludes that 25 percent of all autumnal deer activity

Deer quickly recognize a hunter's patterns. Those who stay on stand longer in the morning increase their chances of seeing deer.

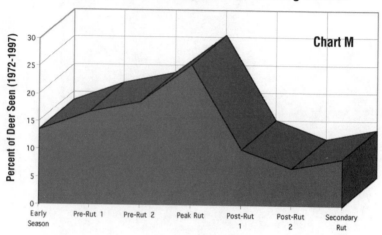

Deer Activity Throughout the Hunting Season

Percent of Deer Seen (1972-1997)

Chart M

Early Season · Pre-Rut 1 · Pre-Rut 2 · Peak Rut · Post-Rut 1 · Post-Rut 2 · Secondary Rut

Time of the Hunting Season When Deer Were Observed

When Woodlen compiled these data on deer observations, above, and compared it with traditional rut-time activity, right, he found his data were on target. For example, Woodlen saw deer activity increase steadily from the early season through the peak of the rut. He then saw rapid declines in activity, which leveled off before increasing somewhat during the so-called secondary rut.

occurs during the narrow window of the rut. That alone is worth remembering when you plan your next deer hunting trip.

Chart N goes hand-in-glove with Chart M. As I stated in the previously, scraping crashes when breeding peaks. What you see in Chart N is an example of this.

Conclusion

For many, this chapter will be helpful in unraveling the mysteries of deer movement. Others will ignore what they find here. For me, Woodlen's insights were revealing, and I found that even though we live a thousand miles apart, our observations have been similar.

Deer Activity Throughout the Hunting Season

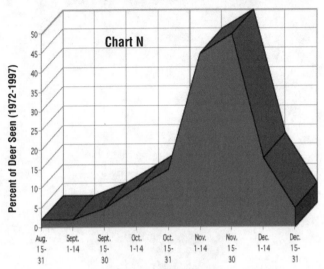

Time of the Hunting Season When Deer Were Observed

This shows how, once September has passed, things begin changing for a white-tailed buck. With October comes a greater infusion of testosterone. This not only changes a buck's attitude, but it also causes bucks to cover more ground. During the rut, it's common for bucks to range from 600 to 3,000 acres or more as they search for receptive does. Near the end of October, bucks make scrapes wherever an adequate licking branch presents itself. For determined hunters like Woodlen, this activity translates into many deer sightings.

CHAPTER 16

Predicting the Future

Russ Price of Pennsylvania has called me at the end of October every year since 1996. I've never met Russ, but I feel I know him. He works on the railroad, and like me, he takes deer hunting seriously.

Each year Russ calls on the eve of his trip to Saskatchewan to find out when he should hunt there the following year. He's seen firsthand how the rutting moon affects whitetail movement, and wants to know when to book his hunts. For hunters like Russ Price, this chapter might just be the most important one in this book, and by itself, probably worth its price.

For several reasons I've chosen to include data since 1995, even though '95 through '98 are history. One of the reasons is to benefit hunters who keep journals and logs. I know the value of each, and I also know hunters like to look back to see what took place in previous years. Another reason is to show the similarities between years.

After analyzing the information that follows, you'll notice the similarities regarding when the rutting moon occurs. By way of example, you'll find 1999 should be similar to 1996. I say this because we have enough data on 1995 and 1998 to know those two years mirrored each other. Therefore, based on this information, '99 shapes up to be a clone of '96. You'll want to remember this as you move through the years that follow.

Where Will It Work?

Throughout this book I refer to the rutting moon as the second full moon after the autumnal equinox. Because of this, nearly all of my writing deals with the area north of about the 40th latitude, which is the Maryland/Pennsylvania border in the East. Actually, the predictor chart that follows, as well as everything else I've written in this book, should work well to about the 35th latitude.

But all is not lost for those living south of the 35th latitude. According to Laroche, the major breeding time will still be influenced by the pre-rut, rutting or post-rut moons, regardless of where you live in North America. One of these moons will be the cuing mechanism. An example is the brush country in far South Texas. For many years I traveled there to hunt and

No matter where you hunt whitetails, the major breeding time will still be influenced by the pre-rut, rutting or post-rut moons. One of these moons will be the cuing mechanism for deer in your region.

When will the rut's seeking and chase phase occur each year in your region? It's not hard to predict this frenzied, important period once a deer hunter knows when the rutting moon will occur.

photograph whitetails. For five straight years it was obvious that whitetails in this region were cuing off the third full moon after the autumnal equinox, the post-rut moon. So, the key in the South is to obtain enough information to know which of the three moons whitetails are using as a cuing device.

What About the "Oddball Years?"

In previous chapters I discussed the fact there are two years between now and 2020 that don't fit my definition for the pre-rut and rutting moons, which are the first and second full moons after the autumnal equinox. Those two oddball years are 2005 and 2013. In 2005, the pre-rut moon will occur Sept. 19, four days before the autumnal equinox. That means that in 2005, the rutting moon will occur Oct. 17. In 2013 the pre-rut moon will occur Sept. 21, two days before the autumnal equinox, causing the rutting moon to occur Oct. 19.

Currently, we don't have adequate data on years when this occurs, because we didn't start getting good data until 1995. The last time there were years like 2005 and 2013 was 1986 and 1994. The year 1986 is so long ago we have nothing to go by. However, for 1994, I've come up with enough journal

Two years between now and 2020 — 2005 and 2013 — don't fit my definition for the pre-rut and rutting moons, which are the first and second full moons after the autumnal equinox. In those years, especially in 2005, it's possible the chase phase and breeding window will occur in mid- to late November and carry over into early December, similar to the way it did in 1997. Only time will tell.

Once the breeding phase of the rut kicks in (i.e., the breeding window), buck activity will continue, but not be as high as it was during the chase phase. Therefore, when scraping drops off, you'll know breeding has begun.

and photography information to know I witnessed and photographed a heavy amount of buck rutting activity the last week in October and also photographed breeding before Nov. 1. Because the pre-rut moon for both these years falls so close to the autumnal equinox, I believe the rutting/breeding activity associated with the pre-rut moon will follow the pattern we've seen to date.

However, there is a possibility, especially in 2005, that everything could be thrown back one month, causing the chase phase and breeding window to occur in mid- to late November and carry over into early December, similar to the way it did in 1997. Only time will tell.

By knowing precisely when the whitetail's breeding period will occur, hunters can accurately predict all other aspects of the rut.

About the Chart

When looking at the chart on Page 217, remember three things. First, if rut suppressants are not a factor, bucks can be expected to increase their daytime activity about three days before the rutting moon arrives. Second, peak daytime buck activity in the form of scraping, rubbing, fighting and chasing should occur from the rutting moon (full moon) to the third-quarter moon (the waning moon).

Finally, once the breeding phase of the rut kicks in (i.e., the breeding window), buck activity will continue, but not be as high as it was during the chase phase. Therefore, when scraping drops off, you'll know the breeding has begun. Also, note that about 70 percent of the adult does will be bred during the breeding window period.

Now, turn the page to find my rut predictions through the year 2020.

The pre-rut and post-rut can offer exciting times in the woods, but I've found that nothing beats hunting the rut during the rutting moon period.

Predicting the Future

Year	Rutting Moon	Prime Chase Phase Period	Breeding Window
1995	Nov. 7	Nov. 4-13	Nov. 14-29
1996	Oct. 26	Oct. 23-Nov. 2	Nov. 3-17
1997	Nov. 14	Nov. 11-20	Nov. 21-Dec. 5
1998	Nov. 4	Nov. 1-10	Nov. 11-24
1999	Oct. 24	Oct. 21-30	Oct. 31-Nov.13
2000	Nov. 11	Nov. 8-17	Nov. 18-Dec.2
2001	Oct. 31	Oct. 28-Nov. 6	Nov. 7-20
2002	Oct. 21	Oct. 18-27	Oct. 28-Nov. 10
2003	Nov. 8	Nov. 5-14	Nov. 15-28
2004	Oct. 28	Oct. 25-Nov. 3	Nov. 4-17
2005*	Oct. 17	Oct. 14-23	Oct. 24-Nov. 6
2006	Nov. 5	Nov. 2-11	Nov. 12-25
2007	Oct. 25	Oct. 22-31	Nov. 1-14
2008	Nov. 12	Nov. 9-18	Nov. 19-Dec. 3
2009	Nov. 2	Oct. 31-Nov. 8	Nov. 9-22
2010	Oct. 22	Oct. 19-28	Oct. 29-Nov. 11
2011	Nov. 10	Nov. 7-16	Nov. 17-30
2012	Oct. 29	Oct. 26-Nov. 4	Nov. 5-18
2013*	Oct. 19	Oct. 16-25	Oct. 26-Nov. 8
2014	Nov. 7	Nov. 4-13	Nov. 14-29
2015	Oct. 27	Oct. 24-Nov. 2	Nov. 3-16
2016	Nov. 14	Nov. 11-20	Nov. 21-Dec. 5
2017	Nov. 3	Nov. 1-9	Nov. 10-23
2018	Oct. 24	Oct. 21-30	Oct. 31-Nov. 13
2019	Nov. 11	Nov. 8-17	Nov. 18-Dec. 1
2020	Oct. 31	Oct. 28-Nov. 6	Nov. 7-20

Oddball years: It's possible these two years could look much like 1997. They're borderline. Refer to previous paragraph for more information.

Reference for the full moon dates: Astronomy With Your Personal Computer, 2nd edition. Peter Duffett-Smith. Cambridge University Press 1990.

CHAPTER 17

Earning the Hunter's Respect

Not long ago, a well-known wildlife biologist said, "One of the problems with outdoor writers who write about deer hunting is that they don't think things through. They jump to conclusions. They go from Point A to D without considering what B and C have to say. Because of this, I don't take much stock in what the average hunting writer has to say when it comes to white-tailed deer. Very few know what they're talking about."

I was so taken aback, I wrote that down before I forgot it.

At first, his comments offended me. However, rather than letting it get the best of me, I pondered what the biologist said. In the minutes, hours, days and months since, I've thought about his statement. Is there truth in what he said about outdoor writers who write about whitetails or anything in nature? Probably. Was I ever guilty of it? Probably, although not intentionally.

Humans have a fallacy in our ability to stretch or exaggerate things. I'm not a fisherman, but I'm told fish are always bigger hours or days after they're caught. I'm sure that during my athletic career, I stretched the distance of a home run once or twice.

So, rather than steam and fuss about the biologist's comments, I've remembered them when writing — especially about the moon research Laroche and I are involved in.

Caution

It's easy to become gun-shy when writing about something new or different than what biologists have written. Also, because my college background is in business administration and not wildlife management, I sometimes feel like I'm in no man's land.

Two people who tilted the table and put me over the hump to write this were Patrick Durkin, editor of *Deer & Deer Hunting*, and Dave Samuel, a retired professor of wildlife biology at the University of West Virginia. They encouraged me to continue with what Laroche and I were doing. Last fall, I lectured at the University of West Virginia's College of Agriculture and Forestry. The next morning at breakfast, Samuel and I discussed the research Laroche and I were conducting. He energized me when he said, "You're on to something

Nature often reveals itself in subtle ways. The phenomenon of how light affects the whitetail's breeding cycle is an incredible part of nature.

very exciting. Whatever you do, don't let the professional critics stop your work. The people you have to satisfy are the hunters. They're your biggest critics." His words were immediately etched in my mind.

There you have it. Two wildlife biologists with Ph.D.s: one chastising writers, but the other uplifting me and telling me to continue and be honest with the public. That's enough to make someone edgy. In the end, you must go with what you believe and hope the public accepts it. At least, that's the way I see it.

Despite what some might think, Laroche and I aren't reinventing the wheel. Others — namely American Indians — were there before. However, this doesn't guarantee acceptance. It takes time and effort to gain respect.

I realize further public acceptance will require more than the four years I've been writing about whitetails and the moon.

Had I not been photographing and writing about whitetails full time for 20 years, I doubt hunters would have accepted and confirmed some of my thoughts. I've always attempted to be honest and forthright with what I know about whitetails. Further, I've tried to convey my knowledge through articles. In this business, you must pay your dues to be

Hunters take their sport seriously. In many ways, gaining their respect is tough.

Had I not known what to expect from the hunter's moon, my 1998 successes might have never happened.

respected. I'd like to think I've paid some dues through the years. Consequently, 20 years of photographing and writing about almost every type of whitetail behavior have given me a platform to share my knowledge of the moon/whitetail phenomenon. One of the joys of this topic is that wherever I go, hunters want to know the latest about whitetails and the moon. That's exciting.

From the Mail Bag

"Nothing happens until something is sold." That quote, from my days of teaching sales and marketing techniques, applies to every aspect of life. Believe me, if the readers of my first moon piece in 1996 rebelled at the concept, I wouldn't be writing this. Not everyone believed what I wrote, but enough hunters began thinking. Some even started studying what I pitched them. Others, who had been onto the same thing, offered advice. It contributed to the learning curve.

This book probably never would have gone to press if not for the people who responded to my writing the past three years. Since 1996, I've built a file-folder of notes, e-mails, letters, moon/hunting logs and related material from *D&DH* readers. Overwhelmingly, most agree

with my writings. Few letters have questioned the validity of our findings. What follows are some of the comments I've received.

In 1997, the rutting moon was Nov. 4. After returning home the night of Nov. 7, I received a written phone message from Roger Kingsley of Columbia Crossroads, Pa.

"Tell Charlie that the chase phase has kicked in, and the bucks are going bonkers here in northern Pennsylvania," he said. "Bucks are running everywhere."

Kingsley was letting me know my predictions were unfolding before his eyes.

Jack Van Tassell of McCain, Pa., provided a similar story. I got to know him in January 1999, when he attended one of my deer hunting seminars near Erie, Pa.

"You really nailed the rut in '98," he said. "I hunted near Sherman, N.Y., from Nov. 2 through 8. The rut was as dynamic as I've ever seen it. In all my years, I've never encountered so much grunting, chasing and fighting. Then, about Nov. 10, the breeding began. Last year was incredible."

Sam Rank of Lebanon, Pa., offered these comments.

"The reason I'm writing you this letter is because I really enjoyed reading your article on the moon and the timing of the rut in the

Planning is a large part of hunting. A clearer understanding of the moon's influence on the rut is helping hunters everywhere become better at what they enjoy.

September 1997 issue of *D&DH*," he wrote. "I've been conducting my own research on timing the rut since 1995, and I'm convinced the rutting moon is the triggering mechanism, as you stated.

"I've seen this firsthand for three consecutive years while keeping a detailed log of scraping, rubbing, fighting, seeking and chasing behaviors. I just thought I'd drop you a line to let you know your research on the rut is right on the money."

David Pulling, a chiropractor from Silver Springs, Md., has written me semiregularly since 1997. He studies all aspects of the moon, from its phases to its positioning, and has some interesting insights.

"Your *D&DH* article on the moon is one of the best I've read in a long time," he wrote in 1997. "I think my deer hunting might have taken a quantum leap. My notes reflect your findings regarding the peek seeking and chasing behavior as it relates to the moon."

Not every reader has agreed with what I've written. Consider these letters, written two weeks apart by Maine deer hunters who hunted during the same time.

"I greatly enjoyed Charles Alsheimer's articles on the rut and moon

It doesn't matter where a hunter lives, because there will be times when predictions won't appear to work. I learned long ago that nothing is foolproof with whitetails.

activity," Martin Schwimmer wrote Dec. 2, 1997. "His predictions on when the rut would occur in mid-November were right on target, and we saw many nice bucks killed about Nov. 15. For me, Mr. Alsheimer's predictions were accurate."

In 1997, the rutting moon was Nov. 14, so Schwimmer took advantage of what I'd predicted. However, George Sawyer of Edd Harbor, N.J., didn't benefit from my writings, even though he hunted Maine during the time I predicted the most activity.

"After reading your article in *D&DH* (September '97 issue) regarding the full moon, we headed north to hunt northwestern Maine Nov. 13 through 22," he wrote Dec. 16, 1997. "With the full moon on Nov. 15 — with 5 inches of snow on the ground, cool temperatures and cloudy conditions — we saw little sign or buck activity. (There were) no scrapes and not much of anything. We were there at the right time and had snow, but saw no sign and no deer. Will you give me your comments on this?"

This is a prime example of what can happen, even when people hunt the same state at the same time during similar conditions. Actually, Sawyer's experience could be attributed to several problems. No doubt, some of the rut suppressors I mentioned in Chapter 12 came into play. Obviously, the No. 1 problem was a lack of deer in the area he hunted. It doesn't matter where a hunter lives, because there will be times my predictions — or those of any other writer — won't appear to work. I learned long ago that nothing is foolproof with whitetails.

Give and Take

These are just some of the comments I've received from hunters since 1996. I even welcomed the negative letters. The positive ones keep me going, and the negative ones remind me I must keep searching for another missing piece to the puzzle. It makes for an exciting journey.

Without hunter input, this process would quickly become stale. The

Without hunter input, this process would quickly become stale.

feedback I've received has shown me where I've taken a wrong turn, and has kept me focused and stimulated. I don't consider what Laroche and I are doing as a one-way street. We have lots of give and take with hunters.

After all, without hunters, there wouldn't be much need for what we're doing.

CHAPTER 18

The Final Word

After scanning this section, you might ask, "What does this have to do with whitetails and the moon?" Nothing in some ways, but everything in others. The 35 mm camera has defined my career. Others have conveyed their messages as hunter/writers or just photographers. I'm one of the few outdoor communicators who is a serious deer hunter and nature photographer. Had it not been for the camera, I wouldn't know what I do about white-tailed deer. The quest for one more picture has often kept me afield when others would have quit. This perseverance has usually let me find a window into the whitetail's world.

So, I owe my profession and knowledge to photography more than anything else. Failing to share some tips and the story behind my photos would leave my book with an incomplete ending.

Origins

It's difficult to say when the photography bug first bit me. Certainly, the seeds were planted when I began admiring Leonard Lee Rue's and Erwin Bauer's whitetail photos in high school. They were pioneers in wildlife photography. I couldn't help but wonder what it would be like to shoot images like theirs. Because of their inspiration, I bought my first 35 mm camera, a top-of-the-line Miranda Sensorex, while stationed in Vietnam in the late 1960s. While there, I was fortunate to be on a base with a photo hobby shop. The shop could process color and black-and-white photos, and during my 14 months in Southeast Asia, I regularly shot and developed my own film. Because many of the military photographers used the shop to process their film, I received tips and learned from their work. When I returned from Vietnam in 1970, I had one camera body and a 200 mm lens, and was determined to begin photographing nature.

I quickly realized that a 200 mm lens was not long enough to shoot the whitetail photos I wanted, so I bought a cheap 400 mm f5.6 lens. Although inferior to modern lenses, it got me started. With that in hand, I frequently shot pictures at a local deer-wintering area my first year home. The experience hooked me.

As I discovered in January 1970, the beauty of hunting deer with a camera is that the season lasts all year and has no bag limits.

Here's my main camera arsenal. I shoot about 95 percent of my photos with these "guns."

I shoot Nikon cameras and lenses, and currently rely heavily on four lenses for whitetail photography: a 35-to-70 mm f2.8, an 80-to-200 mm f2.8 ED zoom, a 200-to-400 mm f4.0 ED zoom and a 500 mm f4.0. All but the 200-to-400 zoom are autofocus lenses. These lenses are extremely sharp and expensive, and they let me photograph in less-than-adequate light.

I typically try to use the 80-to-200 zoom mounted on a tripod or camera gunstock, although I'll shoot it offhand if lighting permits. The 200-to-400 mm zoom and 500 mm are heavy, and I always use them with a tripod to ensure the pictures are sharp.

Film

The color film I use changes with technology. For years, I shot mostly Kodachrome 64. When the film wars heated up, film improved, so I shot what I perceived to be the best film at that time. Nowadays, I use three color slide films: Fuji Velvia (ASA 50) for scenics, Fuji 100 Sensia (ASA 100) for animals and Kodachrome 200 for dim light. I use Fuji Velvia for scenics because it's one of the sharpest films, and its colors

Always try to work the light. Cross- or back-light can provide some dramatic photos.

are incredible. I shoot it at its ASA rating of 50. Fuji Sensia is almost as sharp as Velvia, and I shoot it at ASA 125, although it's ASA 100 film. Kodachrome 200, an ASA 200 film, is sharp for a fast-speed film. I shoot it at ASA 250 for better color saturation. Although I shoot it at ASA 250, I don't tell the processing lab I push it. I have them develop it normally.

Remember a couple of things about film. First, always shoot slide film. Usually, you can make better prints from slides than from print film, although this is changing. Also, by shooting slide film, you'll have slides for projection purposes and, if you're fortunate, possible magazine sales. Second, slower ASA films will be sharper and have better colors. Unfortunately, everything is a trade-off, and using slow-speed film usually means shooting off a tripod.

Equipment

Today's cameras are vastly different than when I began photographing in the late '60s. Except for the light meter, my first camera was an all-manual 35 mm. Today, almost all of my cameras have several programming modes, have outstanding metering systems, are capable of

Back-lit photos of bucks in velvet have special beauty. When possible, I try to set up for a side- or back-lit photo.

Action photos are the toughest to get. You'll need to anticipate the action and shoot at a shutter speed of 500 or faster. If you get one or two good images out of a roll of film, consider yourself fortunate.

autofocus and can advance film at more than five frames per second.

Because of the nature of whitetail photography, the 35 mm camera is the format of choice. I also own several medium-format cameras, but they are simply too large and bulky to take most wildlife photos.

When someone asks me about cameras for photographing whitetails, I ask them how much money they're willing to spend. Today's cameras aren't cheap, and they're loaded with bells and whistles. The more features they have, the more expensive they are.

For the novice to moderately serious amateur, I recommend a medium-priced 35 mm camera body with a good, built-in self-timer and a 35-to-70 mm zoom lens. This lens has a magnification of wide-angle to about 1.25 power, and is excellent for scenics. The lens' magnification can be calculated by dividing 50 into the lens' millimeter measurement.

Most of today's medium-priced camera bodies are as good as top-of-the-line models from 10 years ago. They feature excellent light-meters and often have autofocus features. They also have built-in autowinders, which many call motor drives. These can be good and bad. The good side is that the winder automatically advances film, so you can get to the

I don't often try to add motion to a still photo, but it can show the intensity and drama of what was occurring when the photo was taken. I showed motion — blurring — of this buck rubbing by shooting at a slow shutter speed.

For serious whitetail photographers, a 300 mm lens — or better yet, 400 mm — is necessary for shooting wary animals.

next frame before the action changes. The bad side is that most are noisy and spook deer. Try to find a camera with a quiet film advance.

From Starters to Serious Photography

To start photographing deer, a zoom lens in the 80-to-200 mm range is essential. Also, get one with the lowest f-setting you can afford. The smaller the f-number, the less light is required to take a picture. I have two 80-to-200 mm lenses that are f2.8, and they let me photograph in dim light. People often think most deer photos are taken with long lenses. Many are, but the 80-to-200 mm is my workhorse lens and a favorite for whitetails.

For serious whitetail photographers, a 300 mm lens — or better yet, 400 mm — is necessary for shooting wary animals. A 300 mm, or 6-power, and 400 mm, or 8-power, let you bring the animal close without spooking it. Usually, deer photographs on the covers of major outdoors magazines are shot with 300- , 400- or 500 mm lenses. The downside to these lenses is their weight and cost. The weight of most requires you to use a tripod. Also, the prices of these lenses can make you sick. At today's prices, expect to pay $1,000 to $7,000 for a long telephoto lens. Like other lenses, the lower the f-setting, the better your chances of photographing in dim light. The lower f-setting lenses are also the most expensive.

A sturdy tripod is one of the last pieces of equipment required for deer photography. Although it's the last piece I mention, don't skimp on price. The quality of your photos will be directly related to how steady your camera is when the picture is taken. My lightweight tripod is a Gitzo G1228 with a Slik Pro ball-head. My serious tripod — the one I use for long lenses — is a Gitzo 320 with an ARCA ball-head. It's sturdy and heavy, but worth the inconvenience of carrying it.

Portable blinds aren't necessary for whitetail photography, but they're nice. You can make your own or buy one of the many on the market.

Composition can make or break a photo. Often, I try to place the primary object — the big buck in this case — off-center.

Dollar for dollar, Leonard Lee Rue's Ultimate Blind is difficult to beat. It's lightweight and can be set up in less than a minute.

Getting the Photo

When I began photographing whitetails, I didn't have a clue about what I was doing and learned as I progressed. During those early years, I was more intent on just getting deer in the frame than thinking about composition, lighting or depth of field. These aspects of photography take time to develop. However, with a little knowledge, you can shorten the learning curve.

When composing photos of deer or hunters, I try to think how the subject will look best in the picture. As a result, I often put the subject off-center in the picture so it becomes part of the scene. To enhance the photo's composition, I'll try to find a tree or other object with which to frame the person or animal. From an artistic standpoint, these things make photos better. That is, I prefer to have my photos tell a story. This isn't to say I don't take tight portraits, because I do. However, when possible, I try to get artistic.

When I take portraits of people or animals, I focus on their eyes. The

I love to capture the hunting experience on film because it lets me relive the moment.

eye is the center of attention, and reveals the soul and character of the subject. Also, the glint of an eye adds to the photo. In addition, I like to take photos from the subject's eye level. If your subject is a fawn lying on the forest floor, that means photographing from your belly.

Light is the key to photography. When possible, I try to position an animal or hunter so it's not in direct sunlight. If I have a choice, I'll photograph the subject in cross- or back-light. This lighting makes more dramatic photos.

Perhaps the greatest challenge in nature photography is capturing action. Things happen fast in the wild, and getting things right doesn't just happen. To stop action, you need to shoot at a shutter speed of at least a $\frac{1}{500}$ second, or $\frac{1}{1,000}$ second if you have enough light. Of course, you'll sometimes want to show action by blurring the motion.

Hunter Setups
Photographing whitetails and other animals is what nature photography is all about. However, I love to capture the hunting experience on film because it lets me relive the moment.

Taking pictures of kill scenes in ways that don't offend people is one of the most overlooked aspects of hunting photography. Showing lots of blood or deer with their tongues hanging out repulses many people — especially nonhunters — and projects a poor image of deer hunting. So, photographing this aspect of hunting is critical.

Most of my hunter set-up photos are taken with a 35-to-70 mm or 80-to-200 mm f2.8 zoom lens attached to a camera body and tripod. My camera's self-timer can be programmed to allow two to 30 seconds between the shutter release and when the photo is taken. It's a great feature for someone who hunts alone and wants to take his own photo.

If I'm hunting alone and need to take a self-portrait, the process is easy. First, I program the camera for the time I think I'll need. Then, I compose the photo, press the shutter and move to the predetermined spot where I'll appear in the photo.

Angles can mean everything when photographing a hunter walking

I love reflection photos because of the impact they provide to the overall photo. I believe this adds to a picture's composition.

Always try to focus on the eyes of an animal or person. The eyes are the center of attention, and the heart and soul of the object.

toward a deer. After the kill, I position a deer where I think it looks best, taking advantage of nice framing possibilities. Then, I usually position the camera a short distance from the buck's head, compose the photo and focus on the buck's eyes. If I want the hunter to be in sharp focus, I make sure the lens' f-setting is at least at f8 or higher. If I want the hunter to be slightly out of focus, I'll set the f-setting from f2.8 to f5.6.

If I'm taking a hero shot — of myself or someone else — I make sure there's no blood on the deer. Also, I work the angles, trying to get the best pose. If I'm photographing another hunter with his deer, I focus on the deer's eyes if it's a fresh kill. If I'm doing a self-portrait, things become more difficult. To take my own picture, I check the scene carefully, noting the height of certain branches around the buck. With this in mind, I compose the photo by using the branches as frames of reference so I don't cut my head off in the picture. I then use as high an f-setting as possible — f8 to f16 — so I have a good depth of field, meaning everything is sharp, and take my portrait. It takes time to get used to this, but with practice it becomes rather easy.

It's important to make sure a buck looks like it's a fresh kill. After a buck has been dead for several hours, its eyes glaze and start to become

Capturing the hunting experience on film helps relive the moment.

When composing a hunter set-up photo, try to be low to the ground, and focus on the object's eyes.

sunken. To remedy this, use a pair of glass taxidermy eyes to make the buck's eyes look fresh. They slip in like contact lenses and can make a buck look like it did moments after it was killed. Also, keep the buck's tongue in its mouth, and keep the mouth closed. If the mouth won't stay closed by itself, force it shut by inserting a small nail through the bottom of a buck's jaw and into its palate. If I kill a buck just before dark and want to photograph it in daylight, I gut it out, clean the hair to remove blood and lay the carcass on pallets overnight. The next day, I can photograph the buck after I insert glass eyes. Don't hang a buck by its antlers if you want to photograph it later. The weight of its body will stretch the neck, and the photos won't be realistic.

About the Author

C harles J. Alsheimer was born and raised on a farm in the Finger Lakes Region of New York State. He has devoted his life to photographing, writing and lecturing on the beauty of God's creation.

Alsheimer is an award-winning nature photographer and outdoor writer, and one of the top white-tailed deer authorities in North America. He presents his multi-media nature programs year-round to churches, organizations, civic clubs and public schools across the country.

Alsheimer is the Northern field editor for *Deer & Deer Hunting* magazine. During the past 20 years, his pursuit of the white-tailed deer and other species has taken him across North America. Since 1979 his photos have appeared in nearly every outdoor publication in America. He has more than 100 national magazine cover photos to his credit, and has written more than 200 published articles on white-tailed deer.

In addition, his photos have won numerous state and national photo contests. He is the author of two popular books, *Whitetail: The Ultimate Challenge* and *Whitetail: Behavior Through the Seasons*, as well as the co-author of *A Guide to Adirondack Deer Hunting*.

Alsheimer is an active member of the Outdoor Writers Association of America and the New York State Outdoor Writers Association. He has also served as a nature photography instructor for the National Wildlife Federation at its Nova Scotia, Blue Ridge and Maine summits.

Alsheimer, his wife, Carla, and son, Aaron, live on a 210-acre farm and white-tailed deer research facility near Bath in rural upstate New York.

INDEX

Charlie Alsheimer's Ultimate Deer Hunting Seminar

Each year, Charles Alsheimer presents numerous fund-raising seminars across the country. These are hard-hitting programs dealing with many topics of interest to whitetail hunters, including: scouting, sign interpretations, scrape-hunting, finding wounded deer, quality deer management, rattling and vocalization, hunting whitetails with decoys, hunting whitetails by the moon, ethics and hunting's future — the most important subject — and more.

"Your presentation was terrific! Many in attendance stated that your program was the most professional, in-depth seminar they had ever heard on the whitetail."

— Corky N. Newcomb, organizer
New England Deer Hunting Show and Seminar
Manchester, N.H.

"Thank you for the excellent deer hunting seminar. It was by far the best hunting program that has ever been to the Kane area."

— Randy Durante, organizer
Kane Rotary Club
Kane, Pa.

"A tip of the hat goes to Charlie Alsheimer. His deer hunting seminar and multimedia were outstanding. He truly knows the great outdoors and teaches all how to appreciate what God has given us."

— Patrick P. Domico, secretary
Governor's Sportsman's Advisory Council
State of Pennsylvania

For information about how your group can raise money by hosting one of Charles Alsheimer's seminars, contact him at 4730 Route 70A, Bath, NY 14810, or call (607) 566-2781.

Other Books by Charles J. Alsheimer

For more than 20 years, Charles Alsheimer's photos and writing have inspired and educated deer hunters across North America. Here's what hunters are saying about his previously published books — *Whitetail: The Ultimate Challenge* and *Whitetail: Behavior Through the Seasons.* Both are available from Krause Publications.

"Wow! What a book! I just got your book Whitetail: Behavior Through the Seasons, *and I've had a devil of a time keeping it away from my family long enough to look at it. The photography is incredible!"*

— John L. Conrad
Washington, D.C.

"My library goes way back and includes Advanced Hunting *by Francis Sell,* Whitetail *by George Mattis and* World of the Whitetail *by Leonard Lee Rue. Your book* Whitetail: The Ultimate Challenge *is the best writing on hunting the whitetail I've read."*

— Haas Hargrave
Wayland, N.Y.

"I'm 40 years old and have hunted deer all my life. I recently purchased your book Whitetail: The Ultimate Challenge *and was overwhelmed by your ethics and tactics. I want to compliment you on such an outstanding book."*

— Richard Washburn
Middleboro, Mass.

"I'm an 11-year-old kid who is really into hunting. I learned so much from your book, Whitetail: The Ultimate Challenge. *It taught me that hunting isn't just shooting a buck. It's about being able to be in nature and see the world of the white-tailed buck. I hope you write more books."*

— Jordan Moore
Bowling Green, Ky.

Unlock Secrets To
ULTIMATE WHITETAIL HUNTING

Whitetail Behavior Through the Seasons
by Charles J. Alsheimer
More than 160 striking action shots reveal a rarely seen side of North America's most impressive game animal. In-the-field observations will help you better understand all aspects of the whitetail deer, from breeding to bedding. Nature lovers and hunters will love this stunning book.
Hardcover • 9 x 11-1/2 • 208 pages
166 color photos
WHIT • $34.95

Whitetail The Ultimate Challenge
by Charlie Alsheimer
Here's the key to unlocking deer hunting's most intriguing secrets. Find insights on where and how to hunt whitetails across North America. Plus, Charlie Alsheimer helps you become a better outdoor photographer.
Softcover • 6 x 9 • 223 pages
150 b&w photos
WUC01 • $14.95

Oh Deer! The Venison Cookbook for Beginners
by Cheri Helregel
Wondering what to cook now that there's venison in the freezer? Don't worry, let this new cookbook take the anxiety out of preparing venison. With chapters on everything from incorporating venison into your current recipes to choosing the right spices for a venison roast, this book has the solutions you need to serve up fabulous meals from your hunter's harvest. Nearly 100 easy-to-fix recipes give you plenty of options when cooking this healthy and tasty meat.
Softcover • 6 x 9 • 150 pages
20 illustrations
DRCB • $13.95

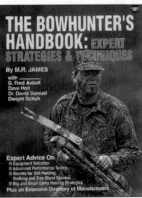

Bowhunter's Handbook
Expert Strategies and Techniques
by M.R. James
with G. Fred Asbell, Dave Holt, Dwight Schuh & Dr. David Samuel
Take your bowhunting skills to the next level as top bowhunters outline stalking, still- and stand hunting North American game from Whitetails to polar bears, with sound advice on selecting the proper equipment, making the shot happen, professional bow tuning techniques and the fine art of camouflage.
Softcover • 8-1/4 x 10-11/16 • 256 pages
500 b&w photos
BHH • $19.95

SATISFACTION GUARANTEE
If for any reason you are not completely satisfied with your purchase, simply return it within 14 days and receive a full refund, less shipping.

Shipping and Handling: $3.25 1st book; $2 ea. add'l. Call for UPS delivery rates. Foreign orders $15 per shipment plus $5.95 per book.
Sales tax: CA 7.25%, VA 4.50%, IA 6.00%, PA 6.00%, TN 8.25%, WA 8.20%, WI 5.50%, IL 6.25%

Credit Card Customers Call Toll-free
800-258-0929 Dept. OTB9
M-F, 7 a.m. - 8 p.m. • Sat, 8 a.m. - 2 p.m., CST
Visit and order from our secure web site: www.krause.com

Krause Publications
700 E. State Street • Iola, WI 54990-0001

Dealers call M-F 8 a.m. - 5 p.m. CT 888-457-2873 ext. 880
for information and a FREE all-product catalog!